"For years I felt that social this book has changed that more, I am ready to create i _____ ......g and now I am more confident than ever that God will help me in my quest."

*Jose Flores, graduate student, UCLA Department of Social Welfare.*

*Jesus for Revolutionaries* is a much needed resource for students who have a passion for righting the injustice in the world around them. Being a U.C. Berkeley alumna, I was surrounded by protests and causes to be passionate about. This book will help students to understand how their faith intersects with their passion for social justice. It is a great resource and I am sure many student activists will be moved by it.

*Donicia Brown*
*U.C. Berkeley, African American Studies, alumna*

"Robert Romero's book is fast-paced, well-researched and subversive. Expertly combining his scholarly background in ethnic studies, personal experiences as an Asian-Latino, pastor's heart, and robust sense of humor -- Romero explores the topic of modern-day justice work in a creative way that challenges readers to re-evaluate who Jesus really was and what he's about in our world today. Read this book and you will laugh, learn, and be challenged to accept the role you play in bringing justice and healing to our world."

*Christena Cleveland, author, Disunity in Christ: Uncovering the Hidden Forces that Keep Us Apart.*

If you have been engaged in the struggle for racial and social justice, seeded in a heart renewed by the Suffering Servant Jesus... if you have ever felt strangely lonely as both a gospel-centered Christian and a kingdom-seeking progressive... if you have searched for voices that spoke the convictions that lead you to your knees in prayer and take you to the streets in protest... *Jesus for Revolutionaries* will speak to your spirit, enflame your passion, and sharpen your vision.

*Paul F. Lai, pastor and doctoral student, U.C. Berkeley Graduate School of Education*

Professor Romero provides an invaluable perspective to the intersectionality of race, class, gender...This book is a blessing for Jesus loving student activists who desire to do God's work and make a difference in the world.

*Iris Lucero, doctoral student, UCLA School of Education*

Dr. Robert Romero, a "Chino-Chicano" offers a revolutionary book from his multidisciplinary Critical Race Theory perspectives that weaves in legal, historical, and biblical perspectives. Incorporating micro personal narratives Romero dares vulnerability, and reinterpreting the biblical texts from the Critical Race Theory lens, he occupies the biblical texts' revolutionary space that counters the ideological use of the texts...The readers will be prompted to join the movement of Jesus for the revolutionaries. Count me in.

*Rev Young Lee Hertig, PhD*
*Executive Director of ISAAC*
*(the Institute for the Study of Asian American Christianity)*
*Organizing Pastor of Shalom Café in South Pasadena, CA*

# *Jesus for Revolutionaries*:

# An Introduction to Race, Social

# Justice, and Christianity

## Robert Chao Romero

Christian Ethnic Studies Press

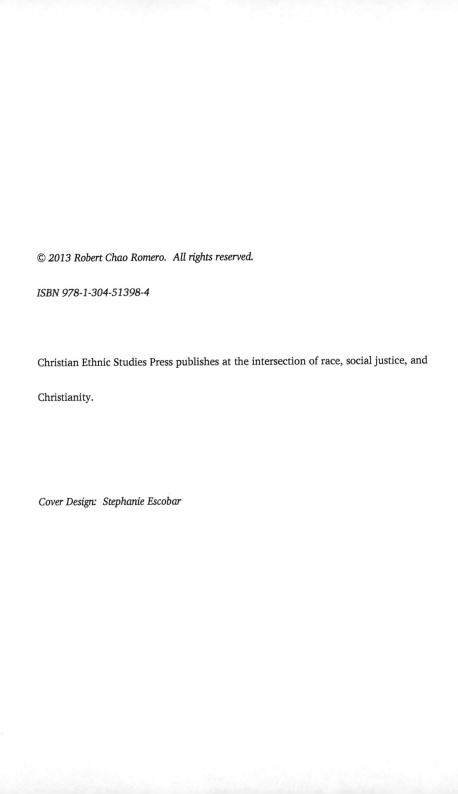

*ISBN 978-1-304-51398-4*

Christian Ethnic Studies Press publishes at the intersection of race, social justice, and

Christianity.

*Cover Design: Stephanie Escobar*

To all my students and colleagues who "hunger and thirst for justice." May they meet *Jesus, the Ultimate Revolutionary* (Matthew 5:26).

# Contents

# Foreword

I went off to college excited about the possibilities of what higher education could afford me and full of ideas I wanted to explore about life. Some of those ideas were about understanding what God had to say concerning the conditions of the neighborhoods or barrios in which I lived -- with all the attendant challenges facing marginalized communities. However I was saddened that the issues of poverty, lack of affordable housing, under-resourced schools, discrimination, etc. were not the issues that concerned my fellow Christian classmates (I attended a Christian college). I felt that God must have something to say, but I was hard-pressed to find anyone in my circle of relationships (even amongst my professors) to enlighten or encourage me. I was disheartened to the point of contemplating that my social concerns would have to be something adjunct to my faith. I wished then that I had access to a book like *Jesus for Revolutionaries*, to let me know that what I felt in my heart and experienced in life were indeed of central concern to God. I finally got there but it was through much toil and sweat (I ended up with degrees in Biblical Literature, Religion and Theology).... and prayer. Prof. Robert Chao Romero's book would have challenged me, inspired me and, above all, confirmed and strengthened my faith in a God who cares deeply for all of creation.

To be upfront and clear, *Jesus of Revolutionaries: An Introduction to Race, Social Justice and Christianity* is a biased book -- biased toward a God who is fiercely interested in the welfare of those on the fringes of society, whatever their status. As an avid student of the Bible, Romero uses his training as lawyer, puts on his hat of a historian and leans on his love of Jesus to provide the reader with a set of lenses to see that justice is integral to God's eternal plan for the world -- yesterday, today and tomorrow. Romero is unequivocal and passionate about his belief in a just God.

As personal as believing in God is, it is not for Romero a private enterprise. It is a belief that is fueled by a faith that is to be lived out in the public arena of life. With the newspaper in one hand, he lifts up current issues that negatively affect the well-being of people of color, and with the Bible on the other hand, he points us to the sacred text that demonstrates a divine mandate to right the inequities in our society, correct our dehumanizing actions to the "least of these." Romero is provocative and even prophetic in his exegesis, to be sure, but nothing less is expected from a revolutionary. More importantly, he is putting forth a clarion call to act, to be agents of justice in a world that is desperate for it. In short, this book is a manifesto of what it means to be a follower of Jesus in a consumption-oriented, violent-prone, polarized world.

Far from being utopian or even sectarian in his approach, Romero invites his readers to engage the process of transformation in very practical ways. He provides a rich trove of resources: links to organizations of all types, books, films, individuals, etc. He identifies helpful networks with which to align oneself. No one needs to go at it alone. In fact, the book provides study questions to ponder with others, in small groups as well as part of personal retreat. These are tools which I wished I had when I felt the Spirit, back in my college days, nudging me to join a movement to make this a better the world, to bring into fruition the Kindom (sic) of God, to be a revolutionary for Jesus!

Rev. Michael Mata
Community Transformational Specialist
Compassion Creates Change

Cheryl Bonsteel
Ron Smith
Audrey Sastak
Walter & Jan Unangst
Vanessa
Maggie
Evelyn

# Preface

This book addresses one basic question: *Can you be a "Revolutionary" and a follower of Jesus?* The simple answer is: *Yes!*

This book is 18 years in the making. In the summer of 1995, I set off to Berkeley Law School to become a corporate lawyer, drive a Ferrari, marry a model, and become rich and famous. Little did I know that God had radically different plans for my life. Through a difficult personal experience (a relationship break-up) one year later, God got a hold of my life. As a result, every dimension of my life was radically transformed. *I found life.*

As part of this life transformation, I began to question my previous ambitions and came to realize that my life had to be more than just about making money and being rich and "successful." At that moment, I felt that God knocked on the door of my heart and told me: "You have never asked *Me* what I want to do with your life." And so I went to a park near my parents' house and prayed: "Ok, God, what do *You* want to do with my life?

That single prayer set me on an adventurous path and led me to complete law school at Berkeley, become a lawyer, get a Ph.D. in Latin American history from UCLA, and, eventually, to become a professor of Chicana/o Studies and Asian American Studies at UCLA. In the process, I discovered my life calling: to study and learn as much as I could about the topics of race and justice. In the university and classroom setting, this means that I research and teach about race and justice through the lens of history, law, Ethnic Studies, and Critical Race Theory. In my personal life, this means that I have a deep desire to understand race and justice from a theological perspective, and to seek deep answers about the following questions: (1) What is God's purpose in creating cultural diversity and the different "races" of the world? (2) If justice and love for the poor are truly at the center of God's heart—as evidenced by more than 2,000 verses from the Bible-- then why has Christianity come to be viewed as a racist, classist, and sexist religion at virtually every college and university in the world today? (3) If Jesus is the God of justice and the ultimate revolutionary, then what are the implications for the way I live my life? *Jesus for Revolutionaries* encapsulates my thoughts and reflections on these critical questions over the past 18 years.

*Jesus for Revolutionaries* is written from friend to friend, one life-long learner to another, in the spirit of Paolo Freire (who was also a radical follower of Jesus). It's written as if we were sitting together over a cup of coffee or a meal at my home, and having a conversation. In fact, *Jesus for Revolutionaries* is based upon many such conversations that I have had over the years with family, friends, students, and colleagues.

*Jesus for Revolutionaries* is not for the faint of heart, and it's not aimed at a mainstream audience. It's written for those of us *on the margins*--students, professors, and activists who care deeply about issues of race and social justice and who often feel misunderstood. Some of us are interested in exploring Christianity, but don't know how to make the connection between faith and justice. Others of us may have

14

grown up in the church, but drifted from the faith of our youth because we couldn't find any Christians who also cared about the poor and marginalized. Some of us have even been criticized by our Christian family and friends for caring so much about immigrants and the poor. *This can be a lonely place.* I know! If you can identify with what I've just said, then this book is for you!

*Jesus for Revolutionaries* is written from my vantage point as a Chinese-Mexican, Asian-Latino, Jesus-loving pastor, lawyer, and professor of Chicana/o Studies and Asian American Studies. This is who I am. This is who God made me to be. This book flows happily and deliberately from my diversity.

One last note of thanks to all those who have journeyed with me and helped make this book possible. I am forever grateful to my friends at New Song Church who steadfastly supported the vision of this book, and our ministry, *Christian Students of Conscience (CSC)*, over the past decade. Thank you New Song pastors Adam Edgerly, Stephen "Cue" Jean-Marie, and Dave Gibbons for your faithful support which played a critical role in the birth of *CSC.* Thank you also Pastor CJ Johnson and Dr. Tatiana Bellanova for playing an indispensable role in launching and leading CSC.

A huge debt of gratitude is also owed to the late Pastor Faye Newman of Los Angeles. She is one of my heroes, and a legend of inner city ministry. I am tremendously grateful that Pastor Faye discerned God's calling on my life and ordained me to the Christian ministry. Special thanks also to my best friend Sam Wu who has prayed, directly or indirectly, for this book every Wednesday night for more than a decade. Sam also did all the time and technologically intensive work which was required to publish this book. Many thanks, Sam!

I am also grateful for our close friends from Navigators and Here's Life Inner City, especially Bob and Susan Combs, Mike and Tonya Herman, and Dan and Nancy Pryor, who have believed in the vision of CSC from the get-go. Thanks also to Randy and Cheryl Lee of Faculty Bridges, who have been my friends and mentors for more than 15 years. We are also grateful for the help of Vanessa Carter who assisted us in putting together the list of resources found in Appendix II.

Special thanks to Caroline Murphy and Hundredfold Ministries who gave CSC a grant to redesign our website. We are also grateful to Matt Eckmann who did this redesigning. Also, thanks to John Hiro Seki who designed the original version of our CSC logo, and big shout-out to revolutionary, Alex Garcia, who further developed the concept for our *Jesus for Revolutionaries* logo and helped us get the word out through FB and YouTube. Thanks to Heber Escobar for contributing your tagging skills to our book cover design, and to Donicia Brown who gave us the idea for our Gil Scott-Heron-inspired cover. A huge thank you to graphic arts designer Stephanie Escobar who fine-tuned all of these ideas and completed the book cover for *Jesus for Revolutionaries!*

I also wish to extend a hearty thanks to Rev. Michael Mata for agreeing to write the foreword for this book. Rev. Mata is a modern-day revolutionary, and one of the leading practitioners and professors of Christian community organizing and community development in the United States. I am so grateful for his mentorship and support which have contributed so much to this book. Muchisimas gracias also to Young Lee Hertig, Jose Flores, Kevin Escudero, Paul Lai, Iris Lucero, and Christena Cleveland for endorsing *Jesus for Revolutionaries*.

In good Mexican fashion, I could not also miss the opportunity to thank all of my family. Dad and Mom, your support over the years is what carried me through law school and graduate school, and it still plays a key role in my life. A warm "saludos" also to my brothers James, Michael, and Richard, my sister-in-law Priscilla, and my new niece, baby Rita.

Most importantly, I owe the biggest debt of gratitude to my wife and love of my life, Erica. Erica was an inner city "revolutionary" long before I was, and most of the truths in this book I learned from her. To my son Robertito and daughter Elena, I love you! You are far more important than any book I could ever write.

Finally, because Jesus said "Freely you have received; freely give," this book is available as a *free e-book*. You can download and distribute as many e-copies of *Jesus for Revolutionaries* as you want by going to our website: <http://www.jesusforrevolutionaries.org/> or to Lulu.com, Amazon, or Barnes & Noble. Our website also features my *blog* and other resources which may help you on your revolutionary journey. The website has more info about Christian Students of Conscience and *the Jesus For Revolutionaries 4-Part Study Guide*.

Just one caveat: *never sell* copies of this book! Jesus already paid the price!

If you prefer an old-fashioned paper copy of *Jesus for Revolutionaries*, you can order one at our website or on Lulu.com, Amazon, Barnes & Noble, etc., too. These we will charge for, but at a slight mark-up above cost. Proceeds will go to support our student ministry, as well as to provide scholarships for AB-540 students.

One significant note. *Jesus for Revolutionaries* is the first publication of Christian Ethnic Studies Press. There is currently no publisher who publishes hard-hitting, ethnic studies books on race, social justice, and Christianity. And so, we felt like we had to begin our own publishing space for this book and others down the road. If you'd like to publish with us, please let us know!

Finally, a brief road map to the book. To start, *Jesus for Revolutionaries* has a lot of little chapters. I hope this makes it more readable and easier to digest. The Introduction looks at the real-life stories of student revolutionaries who fell away from faith because they did not know how to reconcile their belief in Jesus with their passion for social justice. Chapter 1 examines the biblical basis for social justice and argues that more than 2,000 verses of Scripture form the basis for "God's Equal Protection Clause." Chapters 2-5 explore the topic of undocumented immigration and highlight the fact that God loves immigrants and warns against their exploitation. Chapters 6 and 7 put the controversial topic of affirmative action under a critical biblical lens. I argue that affirmative action is not only supported by the Bible, but that Jesus invented affirmative action--for you and for me. At the end of each chapter, we've also included "PraXis Questions" for discussion and personal reflection. "Praxis" is a term which refers to the intersection of theory and practice. We've called our questions "PraXis"—with a capital "X"--to refer to the intersection of theory, practice, and X-stianity.

Chapter 8, "Jesus and the Tea Party," discusses the danger of confusing Christianity with the ideological platform of any political party. The end result of this is always the misrepresentation of Jesus.

Chapters 9-13 are my favorites. These chapters present a biblical framework for understanding racial, cultural, and gender diversity. Drawing from my own experience as a mixed-race "Chino-Chicano," I argue that every human being uniquely reflects the image of God in terms of their personal gifts, talents, personality, gender, and cultural heritage. That's why every person is beautiful--and racism, classism, and sexism are wrong.

I've put on my historian's hat for chapters 14 and 15. Chapter 14 examines the ways in which Christianity has been historically misrepresented as a racist, classist, and sexist religion. Chapter 15 provides the hope. It highlights an important spiritual principle I've found to be true in civil rights history: every time Jesus' name is misrepresented as a justification for racism, God raises up His people to challenge the misrepresentation and to spear-head efforts at reform. If God is the God of justice, should we be surprised?

Chapter 16 is titled, "Modern Day Revolutionaries," and it introduces readers to the modern day Christian social justice movement. As Gil Scott-Heron said many years ago, this revolution "has not been televised." (This is what inspired our book cover). In this chapter, I highlight Christian organizations which are making a major impact in the world today, and my goal is to bring the topic of justice and God's love for the poor out of the abstract and into the practical. I pray that one, or many, of these organizations might grab your attention, and that you can get plugged in with them and start serving! By way of conclusion, chapter 17 asks one simple question: Will you join Jesus' Revolution?

Finally, this book closes with three appendices which I hope will be helpful. Appendix I is a "Faith and Justice Manifesto"; appendix II provides a list of further resources, including books, films, and immigration organizations; and, appendix III is a 4-part study guide which can be used to organize *Jesus for Revolutionaries* PraXis Groups and book studies.

I thank you so much for reading this book. My hope and prayer is that through it you may come to know *Jesus, the Ultimate Revolutionary.*

In solidarity,
Robert Chao Romero
October 5, 2013

# Introduction: Student Stories from the Revolution

*Carlos* was raised in an immigrant Latino community in Santa Ana, California. He first came to know Jesus when he was a child at a local church in Orange County. As a Chican@ Studies major at UCLA he learned about the many injustices experienced by Latin@s in Latin America and the United States over the past 500 years. He learned about the Spanish Conquest which led to the decimation of 90% of the indigenous population of Central Mexico—more than 20 million people. He learned that the conquest was justified by many (though there were notable exceptions) in religious terms, based upon the belief that God had ordained for the Spanish to slaughter the indigenous people so that they might become converted to Christianity. Carlos was also taught about the unjust Mexican-American War which led to the violent seizure of half of Mexico and which was justified by Anglo-Americans based upon a belief in "manifest destiny." Manifest Destiny was the idea that it was God's will for Anglo-Saxon Americans to conquer and colonize North America from "sea to shining sea" in order to spread democracy and Protestant Christianity. Carlos learned that these same settlers created a segregated American society in which those legally defined as "white" received special socio-economic and political privileges, while Latinos, African Americans, Native Americans, and Asian Americans were segregated and treated as second-class citizens. Carlos also came to learn about the structural inequalities within education, healthcare, politics, and law, which have their roots in this historic discrimination, and which persist to the present-day. Sadly, Carlos fell away from the faith of his youth because he came to understand that many of the injustices just described were perpetrated by self-professed "Christians." As a result, *he believed that Christianity was a "colonizer's religion" and that it was a tool of oppression used by white men to perpetuate social, economic, and political hegemony.*

*Elena,* a Chicana single mom, was another student of mine with a similar experience. As part of a faith-based inner city training which my wife and I led for students, she confessed her internal wrestling with God: "The need to be a part of urban justice is huge to me. Being a Chicana/o Studies major many injustices have been brought to light for me. I'll be honest, I have cried many times in class while watching videos or reading books and I have often asked God why...I would like to understand through His words/teachings. [I hope to gain][u]nderstanding and hopefully an answer to the many 'why's' I have. I can cry all I want but my tears won't bring understanding nor change. I recently started going back to church so I'd like to be surrounded by others who also have faith in Christ."

*Regina* struggled with similar internal faith dilemmas, but as an African American woman. She grew up in South Los Angeles and first came to know Jesus when she was a child at her parents' traditional African American church. After finishing high school she decided to attend Cal State Long Beach so that she could become a Black Studies major and study under the tutelage of Dr. Maulana Karenga, the founder of Kwaanza. As a Black Studies major she learned about the many injustices suffered by African Americans throughout U.S. history.

She learned that slavery was justified by many white Americans in religious terms. For example, one commonly held belief of the 19th century was that it was ok to enslave blacks because their dark skin represented the mark of "Cain." Regina also learned about how Jim Crow segregation was condoned by some self-professed Christians who believed that it was God's plan for the different "races" of the world to live perpetually separated from one another. Perhaps even worse, she learned that most white Christians stood silent and apathetic during the Civil Rights movement of the 1960's, and some even opposed Rev. Dr. Martin Luther King, Jr., calling him a communist and "outside agitator." Growing up in South L.A., Regina also experienced first-hand, the many systemic injustices which continue to hurt the contemporary African American community in the United States today. Because she found no Christians who cared about social justice on her college campus she joined the secular Black Power movement. Unfortunately, as her interest in social justice increased, her faith in Jesus diminished. This was because, like Carlos, she believed that Christianity was a racist, classist, and sexist religion which was responsible for the oppression of People of Color.

One last example. *John* grew up in Korean Christian circles and had a real faith in Jesus. He came to UCLA and became an Asian American Studies major. Though his classes, and especially a study abroad trip to Hawaii, he became socially conscious. He learned about many of the historical and contemporary injustices faced by Asians and Pacific Islanders in the United States. He learned about things like the immoral seizure and colonization of the Hawaiian Islands, the Chinese

Exclusion laws, the California Alien Land Law, the Model Minority Myth, and the "bamboo ceiling" faced by thousands of Asian American professionals. John tried to find other Christians at UCLA who understood these issues and who were committed to activism and social change. He found none. And so he walked away from church and held tenuously to his personal faith in God.

*Carlos, Elena, Regina, and John have all had their belief in God shaken because of what they've learned about history, and because of the present-day misrepresentations of many self-professed followers of Jesus.* They've learned the hard cold truth that many of the worst acts of oppression against people of color over the past 500 years have been committed by "Christians." Sadly, they've had this message reinforced through encounters with living and breathing Christians who, often times unintentionally, perpetuate racism through their actions. Tragically, they are not alone. Thousands of students in the United States and throughout the world have had the same experience and have lost their faith in Jesus.

I'm sympathetic to this negative perspective of Christianity. For reasons that will be explained, I don't agree with it, but I do understand it. In fact, if I had not had my life totally transformed by Jesus 17 years ago, I'd probably feel the same way.

This view of Christianity as a racist, classist, and sexist religion is unfortunately backed up by about 1700 years of historical misrepresentation on the part of many self-proclaimed followers of Jesus. As a person who supports his family as a historian, and as a "news junkie," I am all too familiar with these kinds of misrepresentations.    Almost every day I hear about someone somewhere in the U.S. who claims to be a Christian but who says racist things or publically advocates for some sort of social policy which has a discriminatory impact upon people of color and the poor.

*As a historian, however, I know that sincere followers of Jesus have also led some of the most transformative social justice movements of world history.* This inspires me and makes me hopeful.  I've also found an encouraging principle at work in global history:  *Every time Christianity has been misrepresented to the world as a racist, classist, and sexist religion, sincere followers of Jesus have forcefully challenged the misrepresentation and declared emphatically that God is a God of justice and compassion.*  Just as important, they have acted upon these convictions and changed the world.  An important aim of this book is to highlight some of my Christian heroes who have championed racial, socioeconomic, and gender justice over the past 2,000 years.

*Jesus for Revolutionaries* is for Carlos, Elena, Regina, John, and the thousands of students and individuals of conscience like them, who have never received a proper introduction to Jesus, the Ultimate Revolutionary.  This book is intended to be a manifesto and concise manual for them and the many others who care passionately about issues of race and justice, but do not know how to reconcile faith with an abiding concern for social change.  It is also my bold and prayerful hope that this book will launch a global student movement of faith, justice, and racial reconciliation.

*PraXis*

1. Can you identify with the stories of Carlos, Elena, Regina, and John? Have you fallen away from faith, or are you falling away from faith, because you believe that Christianity is a racist, classist, and sexist religion? What are your thoughts after reading this chapter? How do you think God might be speaking to your heart?

Not just Christians but all religions — because they are made up of people

Broaden the gates of love v narrow the gates of judgement

Religion used to justify my theology v explore God's theology

# 1    God's "Equal Protection Clause": The Biblical Basis for Social Justice

The Equal Protection Clause (EPC) is the prime guarantor of civil rights in the United States Constitution. It reads:

> "All persons born or naturalized in the United States, and subject to the jurisdiction thereof, are citizens of the United States and of the state wherein they reside. No state shall make or enforce any law which shall abridge the privileges or immunities of citizens of the United States; nor shall any state deprive any person of life, liberty, or property, without due process of law; nor deny to any person within its jurisdiction the equal protection of the laws."

The EPC was originally created to protect the rights of newly emancipated African American slaves after the Civil War. Basically, the federal government was afraid that states would treat blacks unequally following the abolition of slavery by passing racist policies and laws against them. The EPC was constructed, at least in theory, to prevent the states from denying African Americans "the equal protection of the laws." As we know from history, states blatantly disregarded the EPC, discriminated against African Americans in every

*- the poor ...*
*- the undocumented ...*

horrible way imaginable, and found legal loopholes to justify their racism. Some things have come back around.

Although originally designed to protect African Americans, the reach of the EPC was eventually extended to protect Asian Americans, Latinos, and other minorities from governmental discrimination. In the present-day, the EPC guarantees the civil rights of all people (including whites), based upon race, national origin, gender, and religious affiliation.

One controversy surrounding the EPC is that it has been interpreted by the U.S. Supreme Court to offer little protection to the poor. Poverty is not a "suspect classification" according to the highest court in the land, and the result is that the federal government, states, and cities can pass almost any type of law which discriminates against the poor and it will be found constitutional. With the current conservative shift of the U.S. Supreme Court it is possible that the same might become true for the civil rights of undocumented immigrants as well.

*Thankfully, the Bible has a very different view than the Supreme Court of the United States. The Bible is very clear that any discrimination against the poor and immigrants violates God's Equal Protection Clause.* In fact, the Bible is also abundantly clear that God's equal protection extends to every individual regardless of race, nationality, gender, or socio-economic status. *More than 2,000 verses of Scripture establish the biblical basis for God's Equal Protection Clause.*

A summary of biblical teaching on the civil rights of the poor and immigrants (*God's Equal Protection Clause*) might be summed up in this way:

**All persons born in the world are made in My image, and subject to the jurisdiction of Heaven... No state shall make or enforce any law which shall abridge the privileges or immunities of immigrants and the poor who are made in My image; nor shall any state deprive them of life, liberty, or property, without consideration of My rigorous ethical standards; nor shall they deny any immigrant or poor person the equal protection of the laws. Those who violate My Equal Protection Clause will be subject to divine judgment.**

As expressed by my reiteration of the Equal Protection Clause, Scripture teaches that oppression of immigrants and the poor is offensive to God. At the same time, the Bible is also clear that such injustice is the defining reality of a humanity which has chosen to turn its back on God. As the author of Ecclesiastes states (5:8-11, New International Version [NIV]):

8 If you see the poor oppressed in a district, and justice and rights denied, do not be surprised at such things; for one official is eyed by a higher one, and over them both are others higher still.

9 The increase from the land is taken by all; the king himself profits from the fields.

10 Whoever loves money never has money enough;

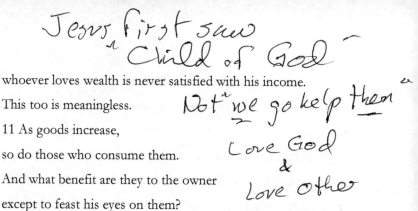

*Jesus first saw a Child of God*

whoever loves wealth is never satisfied with his income.

This too is meaningless.

*Not we go help them*

11 As goods increase,

so do those who consume them.

*Love God*

And what benefit are they to the owner

*&*

except to feast his eyes on them?

*Love other*

In a broken and sinful world, we all fail to love God with all of our heart, soul, mind and strength. As a consequence, we also fail to love our neighbors as ourselves. Because we fail to love our neighbors as God intended, human greed and selfishness rule, and the poor are often oppressed and mistreated. Thankfully, the Bible is also very clear that God loves the poor and defends their cause.

*As we've previously discussed, more than 2,000 verses of Scripture speak about God's love and concern for the poor, immigrants, and the dispossessed of society.* This topic is the second most common topic in the "Old Testament" second only to that of idolatry. (This is because every time people in the Old Testament fell into the worship of anyone or anything other than God, they began to oppress immigrants and the poor.)

In the "New Testament," the topic of the poor and money is found in 1 out of every 10 verses of the "Gospels" (the first four books of the New Testament—Matthew, Mark, Luke, and John— which are basically biographies of Jesus). In Luke, it's actually 1 in 7 verses. Jesus speaks much more about his love and concern for the poor and the devastating consequences of greed than he ever does about heaven and hell (and he does talk about those topics a lot, too).

In fact, the Bible is written from the perspective of an oppressed people group. The Old Testament was written by former slaves (the Israelites) who came to know God by being delivered from slavery and oppression in Egypt. The New Testament was written by "triple minorities" who experienced an intersectionality of three layers of oppression. Not only did they inherit the history of deliverance from slavery in Egypt, they were oppressed and colonized by the Romans and persecuted by the religious leaders of their own ethnicity. An accurate understanding of the Bible must take this important historical context into account.

Here is just a small sampling of what the Bible has to say about God's love and concern for justice and the poor (it would take many volumes to present and interpret the thousands of verses from the Bible which speak of God's love and concern for immigrants and the poor):

In Isaiah 1:17, the prophet Isaiah declares emphatically, "seek justice, rescue the oppressed, defend the orphan, plead for the widow" (Isaiah 1:17, New Revised Standard Version [NRSV]). Later on in the book of Isaiah, the Lord Himself says, "Is not this the kind of fast I have chosen: to loose the chains of injustice, and untie the cords of the yoke, to set the oppressed free, and break every yoke? Is it not to share your food with the hungry and to provide the poor wanderer with shelter—when you see the naked, to clothe him, and not to turn away from your own flesh and blood?" Isaiah 58:6-7 (NIV). In words similar to those of Isaiah, the prophet Amos cries, "But let justice roll on like rivers, and righteousness like a mighty stream." Amos 5:24 (Word English Bible [WEB]).

I love Psalm 140:12 (NIV) which states unequivocally that God fights for the oppressed and upholds their "causa" (cause):

"I know that the LORD secures justice for the poor

and upholds the cause of the needy."

In proclamation of his public ministry, Christ declared, "The Spirit of the Lord is on me, because he has anointed me to proclaim good news to the poor. He has sent me to proclaim freedom for the prisoners and recovery of sight for the blind, to set the oppressed free, to proclaim the year of the Lord's favor." Luke 4:18 (NIV). As Rich Stearns, President of World Vision says about this passage:

"In the first century, the allusion to prisoners and the oppressed would have certainly meant those living under the occupation of Rome but also, in a broader sense, anyone who had been the victim of injustice, whether political, social, or economic. The proclamation of "the year of the Lord's favor" was a clear reference to the Old Testament year of Jubilee, when slaves were set free, debts were forgiven, and all land was returned to its original owners. The year of Jubilee was God's way of protecting against the rich getting too rich and the poor getting too poor." [1]

Can you see where I'm heading? This doesn't sound like blame the poor for being poor, or the political mantra of "trickle down" economics and "equal opportunity not equal economic results." It sounds a lot like "trickle up" justice.

This is also not some radical Marxist saying this, either. It is the Bible and the president of one of the most important evangelical Christian organizations on planet earth.

*God Loves Immigrants*

Many Bible verses also speak about God's love and concern for immigrants. In fact, the Old Testament speaks of the immigrant, or "Ger" (in Hebrew)--92 times! In these passages, God makes it abundantly clear that He loves immigrants, provides for them, and secures justice on their behalf. Immigrants are a vulnerable social group that must not be exploited, oppressed, or mistreated, otherwise God Himself will administer justice for them and curse their exploiters.

"The Lord watches over the foreigner and sustains the fatherless and the widow." Psalm 146: 9 (NIV).

"You shall not pervert justice due the stranger (immigrant) or the fatherless, nor take a widow's garment as a pledge." Deuteronomy 24: 17 (New King James Version [NKJV]).

"He administers justice for the fatherless and the widow, and loves the stranger, giving him food and clothing. Therefore love the stranger, for you were strangers in the land of Egypt." Deuteronomy 10: 18-19 (NKJV)

"Cursed is the one who perverts the justice due the stranger, the fatherless, and widow." Deuteronomy 27: 19 (NKJV)

"Do not oppress a foreigner; you yourselves know how it feels to be foreigners, because you were foreigners in Egypt. Exodus 23: 9 (NIV)

"You are to have the same law for the alien and the native-born. I am the LORD your God." Leviticus 24: 22 (NIV)

"Do not go over your vineyard a second time or pick up the grapes that have fallen. Leave them for the poor and the foreigner. I am the LORD your God." Leviticus 19:10 (NIV)

"When a foreigner resides among you in your land, do not mistreat them. The foreigner residing among you must be treated as your native-born. Love them as yourself, for you were foreigners in Egypt. I am the Lord your God." Leviticus 19: 33-34 (NIV)

More on immigration in chapters 2-5…

*Corporate Responsibility and Labor Rights*

It might come as a surprise, but the Bible also addresses the importance of corporate responsibility. The Old Testament "law of gleaning" speaks loud and clear about this. Leviticus 19: 9-10 (NIV) summarizes this important social justice law which is also restated in Deuteronomy 24:

"'When you reap the harvest of your land, do not reap to the very edges of your field or gather the gleanings of your harvest. Do not go over your vineyard a second time or pick up the grapes that have fallen. Leave them for the poor and the foreigner. I am the LORD your God."

This law from God Himself, commanded landowners, business owners in our language today, to leave some of their potential profits for immigrants and the poor. In those days, when landowners sent out farm workers to pick their fields for sale in the marketplace, some of the harvested grapes and produce would fall to the ground. In this passage, God commanded agricultural business owners to leave this fallen produce, or "gleanings," on the ground so that immigrants and the poor could have something to eat. In addition, this text orders them to leave the "very edges of [their] field" alone, so that immigrants and the poor could harvest the edges for food.

The law of gleaning imparts a very important principle which stands in opposition to the corporate greed which we see rampant in America today: Corporations and other businesses have a moral, indeed divine, obligation to reserve some of their profits to help immigrants and the poor. Corporations should not squeeze as much profit as they can from the hard work of their employees (i.e., the farm workers employed in the above passage) and keep it all for themselves, their stockholders, and their highly overpaid CEO's. This is immoral. Every business and corporation has a moral obligation to give back and not to hoard wealth when millions in America and around the globe are starving. Period.

The Bible is also clear that corporations and employers have a moral obligation to pay just wages to their employees. If they make themselves rich by failing to pay their employees fairly, then, as James, Jesus' younger revolutionary brother tells us, they face fiery divine judgment:

"Look here, you rich people: Weep and groan with anguish because of all the terrible troubles ahead of you.

2 Your wealth is rotting away, and your fine clothes are moth-eaten rags.

3 Your gold and silver have become worthless. The very wealth you were counting on will eat away your flesh like fire. This treasure you have accumulated will stand as evidence against you on the day of judgment.

4 For listen! Hear the cries of the field workers whom you have cheated of their pay. The wages you held back cry out against you. The cries of those who harvest your fields have reached the ears of the Lord of Heaven's Armies.

5 You have spent your years on earth in luxury, satisfying your every desire. You have fattened yourselves for the day of slaughter.

6 You have condemned and killed innocent people, who do not resist you." James 5: 1-6 (New Living Translation [NLT])

WOW! If you've never read the book of James before, you're probably stunned after reading this passage. Whoever makes the false claim that the Bible stands opposed to social justice must never have read the book of James before. I've been criticized for sounding too "angry" in my writing about social injustice—I will now reply, yes, I am righteously angry just like Jesus' brother!

This passage of Holy Scripture is abundantly clear about the moral responsibility which employers have to pay fair wages to their employees. If they fail to pay their workers, and by implication if they fail to pay their workers fairly, they face the danger of God's righteous judgment. God gets very upset when corporations and employers hoard wealth and fail to justly compensate their workers. He is enraged when workers cry out to Him about such injustice. The picture here is that employers who engage in such unjust labor practices are like bloated and overfed cows awaiting the slaughter of God's judgment.

This passage makes me think about the disturbing trend of inflated CEO salaries and unlivable wages for incredibly hard-working, blue-collar employees. Many CEO's make millions of dollars a year while their hard-working employees don't earn enough to feed their families. They benefit from lavish benefits packages and housing and car allowances, while their employees can't take their children to see a doctor because they lack health care. This is not right. This is biblically immoral according to the book of James.

For example, in 2011, Wal-Mart CEO Mike Duke earned $16.27 million, but how many of Wal-Mart's employees could not feed their families or take them to see a doctor? In 2011, the average, full-time Wal-Mart employee earned an annual pay of $15,576. This salary was about $7,000 less than the 2010 Federal Poverty Level of $22,050 for a family of 4. And these numbers apply only to full-time employees at Wal-Mart. What about the many employees who are hired on a part-time basis?

Do you like to travel and stay at hotels? I know I do. Starwood Hotels CEO Frits van Paasschen earned $16.66 million in 2011. How many minimum-wage Latina immigrant moms work at one of the company's hotels like the Westin and the Sheraton, but don't make enough money to provide for their family's basic needs. Be sure to tip big to the cleaning staff when you stay at a hotel.

And do you like the shirts with the little horsey on them? Ralph Lauren earned $43 million in executive compensation in 2011. How many sweatshop workers are suffering in the world today because of those little horsey shirts?

The Costco Corporation is a wonderful counter-example to the rampant corporate greed in America. It is not a perfect company by any means, but Costco gives healthcare benefits to full and part-time employees and pays an average of $17 per hour!  In fact, Costco shareholders were so alarmed by the high wages paid by their company that they actually sued—unsuccessfully--to try and lower compensation rates.  They lost their lawsuit because Costco was able to prove that their fair employee practices led to higher corporate profits.  I don't think that it is an accident that Costco's fair employee compensation policies were spearheaded by former Catholic CEO, Jim Sinegal.  Mr. Sinegal probably read the book of James.

In sum, the Bible is very clear:  It is immoral for corporations, businesses, and employers to hoard wealth at the expense of immigrants, the poor, and their employees.  They have a moral obligation to reserve some of their profit to assist immigrants and the poor, and, for fear of fiery divine judgment, they also have a moral duty to pay fair wages.  Like Jesus' revolutionary younger brother, let's speak out.

*WWDJ:  What Would You Do To Jesus?*

In my opinion, the most powerful testimony to God's love and concern for the poor is found in Matthew 25: 31-46 (NIV):

> 31 "When the Son of Man comes in his glory, and all the angels with him, he will sit on his glorious throne. 32 All the nations will be gathered before him, and he will separate the people one from another as a shepherd separates the sheep from the goats. 33 He will put the sheep on his right and the goats on his left.

*Is Costco a better employer?*

34 "Then the King will say to those on his right, 'Come, you who are blessed by my Father; take your inheritance, the kingdom prepared for you since the creation of the world. 35 *For I was hungry and you gave me something to eat, I was thirsty and you gave me something to drink, I was a stranger and you invited me in, 36 I needed clothes and you clothed me, I was sick and you looked after me, I was in prison and you came to visit me.'*

37 "Then the righteous will answer him, 'Lord, when did we see you hungry and feed you, or thirsty and give you something to drink? 38 When did we see you a stranger and invite you in, or needing clothes and clothe you? 39 When did we see you sick or in prison and go to visit you?'

40 *'The King will reply, 'Truly I tell you, whatever you did for one of the least of these brothers and sisters of mine, you did for me.'*

41 "Then he will say to those on his left, 'Depart from me, you who are cursed, into the eternal fire prepared for the devil and his angels. 42 For I was hungry and you gave me nothing to eat, I was thirsty and you gave me nothing to drink, 43 I was a stranger and you did not invite me in, I needed clothes and you did not clothe me, I was sick and in prison and you did not look after me.'

44 "They also will answer, 'Lord, when did we see you hungry or thirsty or a stranger or needing clothes or sick or in prison, and did not help you?'

45 "He will reply, *'Truly I tell you, whatever you did not do for one of the least of these, you did not do for me.'*

41

46 "Then they will go away to eternal punishment, but the righteous to eternal life."

These words of Jesus present a stunning truth: Jesus loves and cares about immigrants and the poor so much that when we love them we are actually loving him!

Jesus identifies so closely with the struggles of the poor that he teaches that the barometer of a sincere relationship with him is whether or not we love the poor. If we love him, then we will love the poor. When we love the poor we are loving him.

St. Augustine put it this way, Jesus is present "in the person of the poor." "Christ is needy when a poor person is in need" and "is hungry when the poor are hungry." "To come to the aid of the poor...is to come to the aid of Christ the Head who is present and in need in the poor." I love Mother Theresa's summation of Matthew 25, too: "Jesus appears in the distressing disguise of the poor."

I like to describe these verses in Matthew as the "WWDJ," or, "What Would You Do To Jesus" passage. It's common to see people wearing bracelets which say, "WWJD," or "What Would Jesus Do." The sentiment behind these catchy bracelets is a good one. The idea is that, when confronted with a difficult situation, the wearer of the bracelet will stop him or herself and ask, "What would Jesus do in this situation?" "WWDJ" stands for a related, but different proposition drawn from the logic of Matthew 25: If Jesus is really present in immigrants, the homeless, and the poor, then we should think long and hard about the way we respond in our daily lives to immigrants, homeless individuals, or the poor. Would you ever call Jesus a racist name like "beaner," "spic," or "wet back"? Would you ever spit upon Jesus and call him "lazy" and a "bum" if He asked you for money outside of your local grocery store? Would you ever call Him a "welfare mom who needs to stop having babies and get a job"?

The fact of the matter is that if we really take the Bible seriously, then Jesus is present in the homeless person wandering our local neighborhood in search of food and a dry and safe place to lay her head; he is present in the undocumented male immigrant cutting our lawn, cooking our meal and cleaning our dishes in the backroom of Denny's; he is present in the undocumented mujer who cleans our home and raises our children, and, as Cesar Chavez understood, in the farm worker who picks our fruit at minimum wage so that we can buy strawberries on sale for $3.99 at Trader Joe's. Jesus is also present in the "AB-540 student" who works 30- 40 hours a week, commutes 100 miles a day by public transportation, and who sacrifices food for books in order to attend UCLA. He is present in the Mexicana who is deported and ripped apart from her young U.S.-citizen children and deported to Mexico because mainstream U.S. society is content to benefit from her cheap labor and at the same time blame her for all of it's social ills; Jesus is present in the female Asian immigrant who was tricked into prostitution and who now lives as a sex slave in Monterey Park, and in her relatives who labor away in sweatshops of Downtown L.A. so that a sixteen year old suburban teen can buy her trendy jeans on sale at Forever 21; he is also present in the African-American and Latino youth of South L.A. who are denied equal access to quality public education, medical care, safe parks, and so many other things; he is present in all of the  inner city residents of the United States who suffer from the increased risk of a multitude of health problems because they live in "food deserts"; Jesus is present in the many African-American women who experience an increased risk of pre-term pregnancy and infant mortality because of the many expressions of racism which they continue to endure in white America.

Jesus is present in all of the poor, disenfranchised, and "least of society." If we love him, we will love them. *WWDJ*.

*PraXis*

1.      What violations of "God's Equal Protection Clause" do you see in your city, state, and country, or, the world?

2.      This chapter has discussed many rich and powerful verses from God's Word. Did any of them stand out to you? If so, why?

3.      Do you feel inspired to help bring justice to a particular issue in society? If so, what's a first step that you can take to get involved?

1. Unfair wages.
   No access to affordable health care.
   Homelessness & mental issues
   " moved from tent cities
   Immigrants blamed for many problems
      thru-out the world.

   yet - help-wanted ads. WH, rest, others
   . changing cultures; culture clashes


2.  Eccl. 5:8-11   Always been done

   Lev. 19:10   Share
   Matthew 25 -


3.  BES work / F an Conn.
   Vote
   Share experiences ?

# 2    Jesus Was An Immigrant

*Jesús* was a student at one of the best universities on the West Coast. He was a gifted leader, though he was not a follower of Jesus. He decided to run for Vice-President of his university under the sponsorship of a student group which was known for advocacy on behalf of students of color. His main opponent was a middle-class white male who ran under the umbrella of another campus organization which was supported by the Young Republicans. *Jesús* was also undocumented. He had beaten all the odds and made many valiant sacrifices to make it to the university and, now, to run for student office. One day Jesús received a phone call from someone on his opponent's campaign team. Jesús was told: "Watch your back. If you keep running you may get turned in to I.C.E.( the immigration authorities)." This threat was an act of cowardice that would be deplorable to any decent human being. The tragedy of this act however, was that Jesús' opponent was also a self-professed Christian and a member of one of the largest Christian groups on campus. If you were Jesús, what would you think about Christianity?

If I was Jesús I would run as far as I could away from the church and all campus Christian groups. Everything I ever learned in my history books about Christianity being a racist, classist, and sexist religion would have been confirmed in that moment. It would take a miracle to get me to explore a personal relationship with Jesus because of my experience with his followers. Thank God that what is impossible with man is possible with Him.

Jesús' Christian political opponent was not only opposing Jesús, but Jesus. As we discussed in chapter two, Matthew 25 teaches that Jesus so closely identifies with the plight of immigrants that whatever we do to them we do to Him. Any slight against them is a slight against Him. In fact, Jesus was an immigrant himself. Fleeing religious and political persecution at the hands of a ruthless king named Herod, Jesus and his family fled to Egypt as refugees when he was only a newborn. Did Jesus face discrimination as a political refugee in Egypt? What would have happened if Egyptian immigration policy treated the Holy Family the same way that the U.S. treated many Central American asylum applicants in the 1980's and forced them to return to almost certain death? *and now*

Jesus also "immigrated" from Heaven to Earth, abandoning his divine rights and prerogatives to bear the worst of human sin and suffering, that the world might be redeemed and we might be saved.

Because Jesus was an immigrant, maybe this is why He cares so much for other immigrants and teaches that if we really love Him, then we will love them, too. I pray that God would have mercy on me, for I know that I often fail to love immigrants as I should.

Tragically, Jesús' opponent conformed his views on immigration to the political platform of the Republican Party. He also failed to have his heart and mind transformed on this issue by internalizing biblical truths about God's love for immigrants. Tragically, I see this all the time with Christians—both on and off the university campus. I am angered, and saddened, every time. I come across Christian misrepresentations like this on TV., the radio, email list-servs, newspapers, etc.

Not too long ago, I stepped into my car after spending some time in a coffee shop preparing, ironically, for a conference talk about the conflation of Christianity with partisan politics. I turned on the local Christian radio station and the first thing I heard was a political commercial from a Republican gubernatorial candidate seeking to court suburban evangelical voters of Los Angeles. Her message was: don't vote for my opponent because he opposes Arizona SB-1070 and supports amnesty for bad undocumented immigrants and financial assistance for their children who attend college.

I was *disgusted* by this ad because it perpetuated the terrible stereotype of Christianity that we've been discussing in this book. The ad mostly made me sick, however, because it was *mean-spirited, uncompassionate, and contrary to all that I know the Bible teaches about God's concern for immigrants.* It also makes me sick because it assumed that it would find a receptive audience amongst Christians in Los Angeles.

The ad's implicit message was: "As evangelical Christians I know you support Arizona SB-1070. I know you oppose comprehensive immigration reform and any type of social compassion for undocumented immigrants. Undocumented immigrants are bad people. They've broken our laws. We can't reinforce their bad behavior by giving them or their children any type of social benefits. I know you agree. Vote for me." Sadly, this was basically the same political strategy that Jose's opponent used against him. Maybe we heard the same ad on "Christian" radio.

As a side note, if any Christian radio execs are reading this, please be aware of the terrible misrepresentation of Jesus that you perpetuate by playing these kinds of ads. Many of us who love Jesus and appreciate some of your other programming are greatly demoralized every time you mix Christianity with Republican politics. The local "Christian" talk radio station in L.A. is called "KKLA." Sadly, I have heard it called "KKKLA" by one of my Mexican relatives, who, ironically, is a well-known personality on Christian Spanish-language radio. I was reluctant to raise this issue, but too much is on the line for me to say nothing. The reputation of Jesus in the 21st century is at stake. Stop misrepresenting my Lord.

In addition to this radio ad, I was also very disturbed by an email I received from a Christian legal organization called the American Center for Law and Justice. The ACLJ does good work around the issue of protecting free speech in the public arena, but in this case they were off base and completely misrepresented the name of Jesus. In reference to SB-1070, the invidious anti-immigrant law passed in Arizona, the email stated, "There is no question: the debate boils down to political correctness versus the Constitution. And absolutely NO provision of the Constitution is being violated by Arizona's immigration policy." Later on, the email read, "American Center for Law and Justice is a d/b/a for Christian Advocates Serving Evangelism, Inc., a tax-exempt, not-for-profit, religious corporation..."

I am deeply disturbed by this email from the ACLJ because it drags the name of Jesus into the mud. According to the ACLJ, if you are a Christian then you must support the racist Arizona law. What about the fact that the law violates numerous biblical commandments to love and care for immigrants, and not to oppress them (Matthew 25:34-36, 41-43; Deuteronomy 27:19, Exodus 23:9 to name a few)? What about the fact that, subsequent to this email being sent, the U.S. Supreme Court held much of the law to be unconstitutional—its wasn't just political correctness as asserted in the email. What about the fact that the law promotes racial profiling of Latinas/os like myself? What about the fact that numerous Christian leaders have opposed the law, including Bishop Desmond Tutu?

Organizations like the ACLJ confuse Christianity with partisan politics and profoundly misrepresent the name of Jesus. They perpetuate the stereotype that Christianity is a racist, *while* classist, and sexist religion, and, as a consequence, millions of people are hindered from entering into a life-transforming personal relationship with Jesus Christ. Nothing makes me more upset.


*A Positive Christian Witness*

Notwithstanding the horrible misrepresentations of Christianity which we've just discussed, I am very hopeful because of the proactive stance that the evangelical Christian church in America has taken to promote compassionate immigration reform (at the time of writing this, Congress has not yet passed a comprehensive immigration reform measure). I've been waiting a long time for this. I'm particularly inspired by the Evangelical Immigration Table (http://evangelicalimmigrationtable.com/) and its 40-Day "I Was A Stranger Challenge" and "Pray4Reform" (Movement: http://g92.org/pray4reform/).

The Immigration Table consists of a broad evangelical coalition, including: the National Latino Evangelical Coalition, the National Hispanic Christian Leadership Conference, Clergy and Laity United for Economic Justice (CLUE) in Orange County, the Christian Community Development Association, Sojourners, the National Association of Evangelicals, World Relief, Bread for the World, and the Southern Baptist Denomination. In support of their position, they have put together the following "Evangelical Statement of Principles for Immigration Reform":

"Our national immigration laws have created a moral, economic and political crisis in America. Initiatives to remedy this crisis have led to polarization and name calling in which opponents have misrepresented each other's positions as open borders and amnesty versus deportations of millions. This false choice has led to an unacceptable political stalemate at the federal level at a tragic human cost.

As evangelical Christian leaders, we call for a bipartisan solution on immigration that:

Respects the God-given dignity of every person

Protects the unity of the immediate family

Respects the rule of law

Guarantees secure national borders

Ensures fairness to taxpayers

Establishes a path toward legal status and/or citizenship for those who qualify and who wish to become permanent residents

We urge our nation's leaders to work together with the American people to pass immigration reform that embodies these key principles and that will make our nation proud."

Good job Evangelical Christian Table! As an Asian-Latino, Chican@ and Asian American Studies follower of Jesus, I can now proudly say that the church in America has stepped up to the plate to pass immigration reform that is consistent with God's amazing love and concern for immigrants. Yea!!!

To read the original statement and the long list of signatories from many cross-cultural and denominational backgrounds, go to: (http://evangelicalimmigrationtable.com). On the website you can also sign a post-election letter to President Obama and Congress urging them to pass compassionate, comprehensive immigration reform now!

I also strongly encourage you to take the 40-Day I Was A Stranger challenge! For more information and a free "kit" that you can download, go to: (http://evangelicalimmigrationtable.com/). You can do the challenge on your own, or with friends. The first part of the challenge consists of reading 40 different Bible verses about immigration—one a day for 40 days. Along with this reading, you are urged to pray for compassionate immigration reform. As the second part of this challenge, you are asked to contact your local

Congressperson, ask for a meeting, and encourage them to take the 40-day challenge and implement compassionate immigration reform!

As a follow-up to the I Was A Stranger Challenge, the "Pray4Reform" movement creates a community of individuals committed to pray and advocate on behalf of comprehensive immigration reform. To sign up, go to: http://g92.org/pray4reform/.

*PraXis*

1. Can you think of other examples in which people wrongly confused Christianity with an anti-immigrant political perspective? How did this affect you? *75 % of evangelicals support Trump policies*

2. Are you surprised to learn that there are many *But* Christians at the forefront of the comprehensive immigration reform *Robertson* movement? Do you feel led to get involved by taking the I Was A *etc* Stranger Challenge or by joining the Pray4Reform movement?

*Boy, is this out-dated!*

*5. Baptists taking a middle of road approach.*

*Church says one thing*
*Members another*

# 3 "A Day Without A Mexican": The Essential Economic Contributions of Undocumented Immigrants

What if my wife woke up this morning and found me missing—together with my two kids and the more than 14 million other Latinos in California?

That's the premise of the 2004 film, "A Day Without A Mexican." As a means of advocating for compassionate immigration reform, the film shows that the state would come to a standstill without the vital economic contributions made by Latinos—both documented and undocumented.

According to the film (conceived in part by Raul Hinojosa, one of my departmental colleagues at UCLA), Latinos contribute 100 billion dollars to the California economy each year, while only drawing 3 billion dollars in social services. We comprise 60% of all construction workers in the state, and the agricultural industry—the most lucrative industry in California—is entirely dependent upon us. We raise the children of the wealthy, wash their cars, paint their houses, and serve them food and libations in their favorite restaurants.

A lot of us are teachers, doctors, professors, lawyers, and dentists, too.

We (including our undocumented brothers and sisters), pay millions of dollars in taxes which help keep our state afloat in desperate economic times.

And oh, we're not all "Mexican." Though some of us are proudly Mexican, we also come from 21 other beautiful and distinct countries in Latin America—Guatemala, El Salvador, Argentina, Cuba, Costa Rica, Colombia, Panama, just to name a few...

And so, If we Latinos were to suddenly disappear, California would lose out on this wonderful diversity—and also grind to an economic halt. This is the main point of "A Day Without A Mexican."

It's also the main point of compassionate, comprehensive immigration reform.

The 11 million undocumented immigrants of the United States contribute in essential ways to the economy. Recent statistics reveal that undocumented immigrants contribute more than 2 trillion dollars a year to the GDP (Gross Domestic Product) of the United States![1] Without these vital economic contributions, our nation would plunge into economic despair.

Undocumented immigrants do the jobs no one else wants to do—for low wages that no one else wants to get paid. Their low wages ensure big profits for large corporations and small businesses alike, and for the 401(k) retirement plans of millions of Americans. Their low wages also make it possible for 99-cent Big Mac specials, $4.99/lb strawberries, $39.99 Forever 21 jeans, $99 Expedia.com travel specials, and a wide assortment of Angie's List specials.

Undocumented immigrants account for 4.3% of the U.S. labor force—about 6.3 million workers out of 146 million.[2]

They are clustered in construction, agriculture, service sector, and domestic work. Undocumented workers make up:

27% of drywall/ceiling tile installers

21% roofers

20% construction laborers

26% grounds maintenance workers

25% butchers/meat and poultry workers

18% cooks

23% misc. agricultural workers

22% maids and housekeepers

18% sewing machine operators

Note that these are national statistics. In places like California, Texas, New York, and Florida, the percentages are much higher.

To fill our ravenous need for cheap labor, 800,000 undocumented immigrants came to the U.S. annually between 2000 and early 2005.[3] It is estimated that 11 million undocumented immigrants currently live in the United States.[4]

If 6.3 million undocumented workers and their families contribute more than $2 trillion per year to the U.S. economy, guess how many unskilled labor visas the U.S. granted to immigrants throughout the world in 2010?: 4,762.[5] In fact, the maximum number of annual unskilled labor visas granted by the U.S. government is capped at only 10,000.[6]

Can you see the grave injustice here? The U.S. benefits from the cheap and arduous labor of 6.3 million undocumented workers—to the tune of $2 trillion annually–but it is only willing to grant 10,000 (or less) low-skill worker visas per year! The U.S. is not willing to officially recognize the vital economic contributions of undocumented immigrants by granting legalized status and a pathway to citizenship. That's not right! 6.3 million workers vs. 10,000 unskilled labor visas. IT'S A SIMPLE MATHEMATICS OF INJUSTICE!

To fail to grant legalized status to these 6.3 million workers and their families constitutes biblical oppression. The Bible is clear:

> "You shall not pervert justice due the stranger (immigrant) or the fatherless, nor take a widow's garment as a pledge." Deuteronomy 24: 17 (NKJV).
>
> "Cursed is the one who perverts the justice due the stranger, the fatherless, and widow." Deuteronomy 27: 19 (NKJV).
>
> "Also you shall not oppress a stranger, for you know the heart of a stranger, because you were strangers in the land of Egypt." Exodus 23: 9 (NKJV)

Each day we fail to pass compassionate comprehensive immigration reform in this country, we perpetrate biblical oppression and pervert justice. We oppress undocumented immigrants when we allow ourselves to benefit from their essential economic contributions, but deny them the concomitant rights of political citizenship.

The United States also perpetrates biblical oppression when it allows laws like Arizona SB-1070, and evil copycat laws like Alabama HB-56 and Georgia HB-87, to stand. States like Arizona, Alabama, and Georgia benefit in important ways from the economic contributions made by undocumented immigrants, yet, at the same time they scapegoat undocumented immigrants for many of the country's social ills. *This is biblical oppression, too.*

As revolutionaries for Jesus, we must do all we can to advocate for compassionate and comprehensive immigration reform. We must also ask God to carry out *His justice* for undocumented immigrants.

*PraXis*

1.      Are you surprised that immigrants make such vital economic contributions to the United States—to the tune of $2 trillion annually!!! Why do you think that this, and similar statistics are not often discussed in the media or in political circles?

2.      Thank an immigrant for their vital economic contributions. Give them an extra big tip at a restaurant, hotel, or one of the other many places where their work is undervalued and unappreciated. What other ways can you think of to express gratitude towards immigrants for their economic contributions?

# 4    "Secure Communities" Destroys Immigrant Families

Since the horrific terrorist attacks of 9/11, the United States government has continually criminalized undocumented immigrants as scapegoats for the "war on terror." ICE (Immigration and Customs Enforcement) was created in 2003 through a merger of the Immigration and Naturalization Service and sections of the U.S. Customs Service, and its stated mission is to "promote homeland security and public safety through the criminal and civil enforcement of federal laws governing border control, customs, trade, and immigration."[1] Even though none of the perpetrators of 9/11 were undocumented, ICE has systematically targeted undocumented immigrants and their families for deportation over the past decade. In the decade following 9/11, 2.3 million deportation cases were heard in immigration courts.[2] This translates into a 45% increase in deportation proceedings, and it is quite possible that more than 2 million immigrants will have been deported under the watch of the Obama administration by the time our 44th president leaves office.[3] Latino, Asian, and other immigrant groups have become scapegoats in the war on terror.

Such scapegoating of immigrants in times of war, or perceived threat of war, is a common biblical and historical pattern. We are told in the book of Exodus, for example, that the Israelites were enslaved by the Egyptians because they were perceived to pose a potential war-time threat: "Then a new king…came to power in Egypt. 'Look,' he said to his people, 'the Israelites have become far too numerous for us. Come, we must deal shrewdly with them or they will become even more numerous and, if war breaks out, will join our enemies, fight against us and leave the country.'" Exodus 1: 8-10 (NIV). Another historical example of immigrant scapegoating in time of war involved the Japanese-American community during WWII. In 1942, the U.S. government forced 110,000 Japanese and Japanese-Americans to relocate to War Relocation Camps, without due process of law, because it made the one-sided determination that the Japanese-American community posed a war-time threat.[4] Despite this discriminatory treatment, thousands of Japanese-Americans fought bravely on behalf of the United States in segregated units of the Armed Forces.

The so-called "Secure Communities" program represents yet another unfortunate historical example of immigrant scapegoating during time of war—in this case the U.S. "war on terror." As part of this program, ICE seeks to promote "secure communities" by identifying and deporting "criminal aliens…who pose a threat to public safety."[5] To assist ICE in the identification of "criminal aliens," the FBI automatically sends ICE the fingerprints of individuals booked into state and local jails. The FBI receives these fingerprints from local law enforcement officials. ICE checks the fingerprints it receives against immigration databases as a means of identifying individuals who are unlawfully present in the United States.

Although the Secure Communities program might seem reasonable at first glance to some, upon deeper evaluation it becomes apparent that it is fatally flawed. Secure Communities is problematic for three major reasons: (1) it wrongly criminalizes the undocumented immigrant community in the mind of the general public; (2) contrary to the stated goal of targeting high level criminal offenders, the vast majority of those deported under Secure Communities have never been convicted of a crime or have been convicted of low-level crimes such as driving without a license; and, (3) it hurts law enforcement efforts by discouraging the reporting of crime.

By its name alone, the Secure Communities program perpetuates the false, yet common stereotype that undocumented immigrants are "criminals." The statistics prove otherwise and show that immigrants in the United States are actually far less likely than the native-born to commit crime. On a national level, U.S.-born men ages 18-39 are five times more likely to be incarcerated than their immigrant peers.[6] In California, among men ages 18-40, the statistics are even more striking—those born in the U.S. are 10 times more likely to be incarcerated than their immigrant counterparts.[7] The vast majority of immigrants—both documented and unauthorized—are hard working people who contribute trillions of dollars to the national economy and who come to this country in order to provide for their families.

The Secure Communities initiative has also failed in its efforts to target violent criminal offenders. More than half of those deported under Secure Communities have never been convicted of a crime or have only been convicted for a minor offense, including traffic violations[8]. On a national level 1 in 4 people deported under Secure Communities have no criminal convictions.[9] In certain areas such as

Boston, and parts of California, the number stands at more than 50%! ICE head John Morton admitted this policy inconsistency in a public statement: "[Secure Communities] has also identified a large number of lesser offenders and that is because the single largest class of offenders are misdemeanors – that is the biggest pool that you would be identified by a fingerprint program," Morton said, "So we do very much prioritize our efforts but we also don't look away on other people that are referred to us."[10]

Finally, Secure Communities is problematic because it hurts law enforcement efforts. According to law enforcement officials such as Sheriff Mike Hennessey of San Francisco, Secure Communities discourages the reporting of crime because it creates a relationship of fear between local law enforcement and the undocumented immigrant community:

"As the sheriff of San Francisco for more than 30 years, I know that maintaining public safety requires earning community trust. We rely heavily on the trust and cooperation of all community members - including immigrants - to come forward and report crimes, either as victims or as witnesses. Otherwise, crimes go unreported - and this affects everyone, citizens and noncitizens alike. It also leads to "street justice," in which residents who are too afraid to go to the police decide to take justice into their own hands, often with deadly result."[11]

Put quite simply, immigrants fear that they will get deported if they report a crime. Unfortunately, this fear is grounded in real-life experience. My friend's uncle was deported after reporting that his house was broken into during the middle of the night. Someone broke in, so my friend's uncle defended himself and called the police. End result: my friend's uncle was reported to ICE and deported! According to other accounts I've read, a woman was sent to ICE after telling police that she had found a dead body[12] and another young woman was sent into deportation proceedings after reporting that she had been a victim of domestic violence for three years.[13]

In sum, secure communities promotes the criminalization and scapegoating of immigrants and has failed to meet its stated goals. The end result has been the devastation of thousands of immigrant families through the deportation and forced separation of fathers, mothers, and their children. May we, as followers of Jesus, do our part to stand in the gap and speak up against this unjust social policy.

PraXis

1. Can you think of other historical examples in which ethnic minority groups have been scapegoated during a time of war?

2. Contact the President, your local Congressperson, and U.S. Senator, and request that the Secure Communities program be ended.

How to Contact the President:

www.whitehouse.gov/contact

House of Representatives Directory:

http://www.house.gov/representatives/

U.S. Senators Directory:

www.senate.gov/general/contact_information/senators_cfm.cfm

# 5    God Loves "Dreamers": Undocumented Youth and Comprehensive Immigration Reform

It is immoral to deny a university education, and a pathway to citizenship, to the children of undocumented immigrants. Although this may be a popular position in places like Arizona and Alabama, such a denial of educational opportunity and civil rights is utterly unbiblical and unjust.

A fundamental biblical principle is that no one should be punished for an action for which they had no control (Deuteronomy 24:16). To use a biblical analogy, if the parents eat sour grapes the children's teeth should not be set on edge (Jeremiah 31:29-30 NIV):

> 29 "In those days people will no longer say,
> 'The parents have eaten sour grapes,
>     and the children's teeth are set on edge.'
> 30 Instead, everyone will die for their own sin; whoever
> eats sour grapes—their own teeth will be set on edge.

In the same way, undocumented college students should not be punished for crossing a border when they had no decision in the matter.

The U.S. Supreme Court acknowledged this moral truth in 1982 when it ruled that undocumented children could not be denied a K-12 education:

"[V]isiting . . . condemnation on the head of an infant is illogical and unjust. Moreover, imposing disabilities on the . . . child is contrary to the basic concept of our system that legal burdens should bear some relationship to individual responsibility or wrongdoing. Obviously, no child is responsible for his birth, and penalizing the . . . child is an ineffectual — as well as unjust — way of deterring the parent (Plyler v. Doe, 1982)[1]."

Most undocumented college students were brought to the United States when they were just small children or infants. In fact, 65,000 such undocumented students graduate from high school each year in the United States.[2] Many of them are valedictorians and at the top of their class. Tragically, thousands of these students are denied a college education because of state laws which bar them from the university. Georgia, Alabama, and South Carolina all ban undocumented students from attending public colleges and universities.

Although undocumented students are allowed to attend public colleges and universities in most states, most of them find it very difficult to pursue their education because they are forced to pay exorbitant international student fees or are barred from receiving financial aid.

Some states do make it easier for undocumented students to pursue their higher education by allowing them to pay in-state tuition fees. In fact, except for Florida and Arizona, most major immigrant receiver states (e.g., California, New York, and Texas) have passed laws which allow undocumented students to pay in-state tuition fees if they meet certain residency requirements.[3] Tragically, Arizona, Colorado,

Georgia, and Indiana have explicitly barred undocumented students from receiving in-state tuition.[4]

In addition to allowing students to qualify for in-state tuition, California, Illinois, New Mexico, and Texas are among the few states that give undocumented students access to financial aid.

Outside of California, Illinois, New Mexico, and Texas, undocumented students are denied access to public scholarships and financial aid, and, as a result, very few undocumented students attend college or university on a national level. Although 2.1 undocumented youth might qualify for the Federal Dream Act, and 65,000 undocumented students graduate from high school every year, it is estimated that only between 7,000 and 13,000 undocumented students are currently enrolled in colleges and universities throughout the United States.[5]

As a professor of ethnic studies at UCLA, I have found that some of my best students are "Dreamers" (undocumented youth). They are my heroes. They often work 30-40 hours a week, commute 100 miles a day on public transportation, experience quasi-homelessness, sleep in their cars, and skip meals so that they can pay for their education. Moreover, for those who graduate from UCLA, their professional choices and opportunities to attend graduate school are extremely limited because of their legal status. They teach me so much about biblical perseverance and hope as talked about by the Apostle Paul in Romans 5: 3-5.

I am proud to say that undocumented students at UCLA have spear-headed important national advocacy efforts on their own behalf.

In a book titled, *Underground Undergrads*, they shared openly about their struggles as undocumented students:

"Many…[undocumented students]…have described their experience at UCLA as feeling invisible. Students like Grecia leave right when class ends to catch a two-hour bus ride back to South Central where she then picks up her younger siblings from school and heads home to help them with their homework. She works with her mother the days that she is not in class at a sewing factory. Other students live by campus, because they are not able to commute. With her family over 200 miles away, Arlette must balance her full time class schedule with her heavy work load of up to 32 hours per week to pay for living and academic expenses from her own pocket. Still, other students like Linett are forced to withdraw indefinitely from UCLA to work full time in low wage jobs in hopes to save enough money for the following quarter."[6]

To purchase a copy of *Underground Undergrads*, see: http://www.labor.ucla.edu/publications/books/underground.html

To get a copy of the sequel, titled, *Undocumented and Unafraid*, go to: http://books.labor.ucla.edu/p/79/undocumentedunafraid

If you or someone you know is an undocumented college student, check out the following website sponsored by the organization IDEAS at UCLA. This website will provide you with many resources to help you in your educational journey: http://ideasla.org/index/

For all of these reasons, it is a biblical and moral imperative for Congress to pass a version of Comprehensive Immigration Reform which provides a pathway to citizenship for undocumented youth. This is just and right. As followers of Jesus, we must do all we can to make sure that this happens. We must act, pray, and organize. This is what He would have us do.

*The Tragedy of Joaquin Luna*

The suffering of undocumented youth is not theoretical. To make this point clear I would like to close this chapter by sharing about the tragic story of Joaquin Luna.[7] Joaquin was an 18-year old senior at Juarez Lincoln High School in Mission, Texas. He had aspirations of going to college and becoming an engineer so that he could improve his family's life. Because of the failure of the Dream Act to pass in Congress, Joaquin lost hope. On Friday, November 25, 2011 around 9 p.m., he dressed up in a suit and tie, kissed his family, and shot himself in the restroom with a small handgun. Joaquin left suicide letters indicating that he was troubled by his immigration status.

One of Joaquin's letters was addressed to Jesus Christ. In it, he prayed:

"Jesus…I've realized that I have no chance in becoming a civil engineer the way I've always dreamed of here … so I'm planning on going to you and helping you construct the new temple in heaven."[8]

Suicide is never the right response for any of us, but this tragedy reveals the incredible desperation and lack of hope that many undocumented students feel. As Proverbs 13:12 (NIV) states: "Hope deferred makes the heart sick, but a longing fulfilled is a tree of life." Tragically, two million undocumented students in the United States are currently trapped in a legal, political, and social limbo with little hope because of the failure of Congress to pass Comprehensive Immigration Reform and the Dream Act.

May we pause and reflect upon the terrible tragedy of Joaquin's passing. May we dignify his memory by making sure that his story is told, and by doing all within our power to pass Comprehensive Immigration Reform.

Despite my personal sadness and grief over the tragic passing of Joaquin Luna, I am comforted by one thing—I know that God Himself will bring justice for my students and the thousands of "Dreamers" in the United States. Jesus loves them and He promises to do this: "A bruised reed he will not break, and a smoldering wick he will not snuff out, till he leads justice to victory" (Matthew 12:20 NIV).

*PraXis*

1.      Do you know any "Dreamers"? Be their friend. *No*

2.      Contact your local undocumented student group on campus. Come along side them, and ask how you can learn from them and help provide support.

3.      Create a "safe space" for Dreamers on your college campus. Organize several meals during the year in which you invite Dreamers to come and enjoy good food and company—no strings attached.

4.    Raise funds for scholarships for Dreamers.

5.    Get involved with G92 to help organize for Comprehensive Immigration Reform: http://g92.org/

# 6    Jesus Invented Affirmative Action

Jesus wasn't just an immigrant; *He also invented affirmative action.*
*Let me explain.* He believed in those others

What if the only people who could study and teach the Bible
~~gave up on~~
were "Sons of the American Revolution" whose ancestors came on the
Mayflower, and those who scored 1590 on the SAT, graduated summa
cum laude from Harvard or Berkeley, and then received a Ph.D in
religious philosophy from Yale or Princeton? How many of us would
be allowed to study the Scriptures, teach the Bible, and play an
important role in our local church ?

That's not too far from what it was like in Jerusalem in Jesus'
day before He burst onto the religious scene 2,000 years ago.

At that time, the privilege of being a disciple of a rabbi or
religious teacher was reserved for Jewish men who had the best grades
and who scored the highest on the PAT (Palestine Achievement Test)!

In Jesus' day only the smartest and brightest Jewish men
became disciples (students) of a Rabbi. They became disciples by
successfully navigating a three-tiered religious educational system. The
three levels of Jewish education were called: Bet Sefer (House of the
Book), Bet Talmud (House of Learning), and Bet Midrash (House of
Study). Notwithstanding its exclusivity, it was an amazing educational
system for its day.[1]

Male students started off in Bet Sefer at the age of six. Bet
Sefer was kind of like our version of compulsory public education

today.  Most boys were allowed to attend, and the goal of Bet Sefer was for students to learn as much as possible about the Torah Shebichtav, or the "Torah that is written."[2]  The Torah was viewed as the key to life and education was held in such high esteem that Jewish historian Josephus stated, "Above all else we pride ourselves on the education of our children."  This was quite an amazing system of public education for its day.

Students learned about the Torah by memorizing the first five books of the Bible  —Genesis, Exodus, Leviticus, Numbers, and Deuteronomy!  By the age of ten, Bet Sefer students learned all of these books by heart!  That sounds hard enough right, but only those considered "gifted" were allowed to move on to the next level–Bet Talmud.

Bet Talmud took things up a few notches and required students to memorize the rest of the Old Testament!  Yes, 34 more books!  Joshua, Judges, Ruth, 1st and 2nd Samuel, all the Psalms, all the big and small prophetic books…

As tough as Bet Talmud sounds, the big prize was to make it to the next step and get accepted into Bet Midrash, or House of Study. This was like getting into Harvard or Stanford or Princeton.  Only the best of the best made it to Bet Midrash.  Bet Midrash meant you got to study as a "disciple" of a well-known rabbi and this put you on track to become a rabbi yourself.  Being a rabbi was one of the most revered and well-respected positions one could hold.  Think brain surgeon or corporate law partner in our day and time.  As religious and community leaders, Rabbis were at the top of the totem pole.

You applied for Bet Midrash at the age of 14. Getting into Bet Midrash was elitist however, like my opening example. It limited special knowledge of God and the Bible only to those who were deemed "gifted" by the religious and educational establishment. It's as if only those kids who went to the equivalent of fancy prep schools that cost $30,000 a year, aced the SAT, got a 4.7 gpa, and got accepted to Harvard could study the Bible and become religious teachers. If the educational administration didn't think you were good enough to move on to Bet Sefer or Bet Talmud, then you would be sent home to learn the family trade. You got pushed out of the "Israeli educational pipeline" and your destiny was to join the working classes as a fisherman, carpenter, shepherd, etc. Even more significantly, you were excluded from becoming a disciple of a rabbi and acquiring a rich spiritual education.

As part of the application process for Bet Midrash, an aspiring rabbi-to-be would approach a well-known rabbi and say, "Rabbi, I want to be your disciple." The Rabbi would then grill him with theological questions of various kinds. If the student passed the test, guess what the Rabbi would tell him? "Come, follow me." (Do you see where I'm headed with this?)

At that moment a sacred bond was formed between rabbi and disciple. The disciple, or student, was required to leave his father, mother, family, friends, and community—everything—to follow the rabbi. From that point on the disciple's main task was to learn from the rabbi and become like him. The main way this was accomplished was by spending every waking moment with the rabbi. In fact, we are told that disciples would follow their rabbis so closely that at the end of the day they would literally be covered in dust from their teacher's feet. A saying was even circulated among disciples which admonished them to "cover yourself with the dust of your rabbi's feet."

Following 16 years of apprenticeship with a rabbi, Bet Midrash was completed and, at the age of 30 (sound familiar?), one could begin their own career as a rabbi. As a full-fledged rabbi you could then train up your own students, or, disciples.

It is likely that Jesus' inner circle of twelve disciples was comprised entirely of rabbinic school drop-outs, or "push-outs." (As someone who was not allowed into the gifted program of my elementary school called "GATE," I take hope in this. I literally had the "gate" of gifted education closed to me). St. Peter, the "rock," and St. John, "the disciple who Jesus loved" had all been "pushed out" out of the rabbinic school educational pipeline and were not deemed worthy of furthering their religious education. This was why they had to join their dads and become fishermen.

Jesus broke all the rules when He told Peter, Andrew, James, and John: "Come, follow me."

*You could even say that at that moment He invented affirmative action.*

According to the humanly-constructed educational admissions standards of the day, Peter, Andrew, and the rest did not deserve to advance within the educational pipeline of the day. They hadn't gotten the right grades nor gotten high enough scores on standardized tests. They didn't come from the right neighborhood, either. Jesus, Peter, and most of Jesus' first disciples came from "Galilee" which was kind of like "the hood" to the urban dwellers of Jerusalem. Galilee was looked down upon as a region where many "mixed-race" people lived and where orthodox religious practices had become watered down. (South or East L.A. are probably good modern parallels). Jesus came from a town in Galilee called "Nazareth" which may have been one of the most despised towns of Galilee (Perhaps the way many, incorrectly I might add, view Compton or Bakersfield). Jesus, the Savior of the world and God in the flesh, was raised in the hood and chose inner city drop-outs to lead the most powerful and transformative social movement which the world has ever seen. How the Christian church has strayed so far from its roots!

Jesus also broke from the gendered and racial norms of His time as well. You could say that Jesus invented gender and race-based affirmative action as well! Before He ascended to heaven, Jesus told His inner city, rabinnic-school flunkies:

"…[G]o and make disciples of all the nations, baptizing them in the name of the Father and the Son and the Holy Spirit. Teach these new disciples to obey all the commands I have given you. And be sure of this: I am with you always, even to the end of the age."(Matthew 28: 19-20, NLT).

In this passage, Jesus makes a dramatic and literally, earth-shattering announcement to His first students: He says that the call to spiritual discipleship should no longer be limited to males of any particular ethnic or national background.

Jesus, the rabbi and Savior, invites all people—male or female, from every nation of the world, and every socio-economic background– to be His disciples. We all have equal access to the "Jesus educational pipeline." Everyone is invited to be His student. It doesn't matter where we were born, where we grew up, or whether or not we have "papers." Jesus doesn't care what schools we did or did not attend, whether we were in honors classes, or whether or not we ever even heard of the SAT. It doesn't matter to Jesus what we do for a living or what income tax bracket we are a part of. It doesn't matter what ethnic background we come from or whether we are a man or woman. Jesus loves us all and calls us all to be His students.

Like the early disciples He calls us to follow Him and to make everything else in life a distant second—so that we might live in intimate and personal relationship with Him and find TRUE LIFE. As we live as His students and apprentices on a daily basis, He transforms every dimension of our lives and we receive TRUE LIFE in Him. And then He sends us out to change the world.

To be Jesus' disciples is an incredible privilege that we should never take lightly or take for granted. Not only because it is the only path to true life, but also because Jesus broke all the rules to make this possible for us.

*He invented affirmative action so that we might all come to know Him.*

*PraXis*

1.     Have you ever made the decision to follow Jesus as His student or disciple? He's calling you: "Come, follow me."

2.     Have you ever had the experience of following Jesus so closely that you are symbolically "covered with the dust of His feet" by the end of the day? Jesus calls us all to walk in this amazing closeness and intimacy with Him. Try it.

# 7    The Case for Affirmative Action Today

"Our desire is not that others might be relieved while you are hard pressed, but that there might be equality." 2 Corinthians 8:13 (NIV)

Because Jesus invented affirmative action in His own day, I have a hard time believing He would oppose affirmative action in the present. In fact, for reasons we'll discuss later on in this chapter, I have a strong biblical basis to believe that He would be a strong advocate of affirmative action in the 21st century.

The statistical evidence is incontrovertible—we have two types of public education systems in this country: one for the rich who can afford to live in suburbia and go to high-achieving public schools, and another for the poor and largely students of color, who are legally required to attend their local under-achieving public schools. In fact, much higher percentages of Latino (35%), African American (33%), and Native American (25%) students attend high-poverty schools than their white counterparts (4%).[1] 16 million children live in poverty in the United States, and their zip code, not their talent, is most directly shaping their chances for educational success.[2]

Kids born in poverty are 50% less likely to graduate from high school than children from more affluent backgrounds.[3] Those who do graduate come out of their 12 years of education with, on average, an 8th grade skill level. Only 1 in 10 low-income students will graduate from college.[4] Spending in the richest 5% of schools is more than double the spending in the poorest 5% of schools.    On average, schools spend $900 less each year on students from low-income school districts as opposed to rich ones.   $614 less is spent per student in school districts that are predominantly comprised of students of color, as opposed to school districts which are majority white.[5]  A report by Education Trust tells us that 36 states have a funding gap[6]!

The well-known education advocacy group Teach for America highlights the devastating consequences of educational inequity in the United States:

"In America today, educational disparities limit the life prospects of…children growing up in poverty, impacting their earning potential, voter participation, civic engagement, and community involvement.   These disparities disproportionately impact African-American, Latino/Hispanic, and Native American children, who are three times as likely to live in a low-income area."[7]

One recent study conducted by my colleagues Tara Yosso (UCSB) and Daniel Solorzano (UCLA) revealed the grave educational disparities between Mexican American students and their wealthier white peers.   In their important 2006 study titled, "Leaks in the Chicana/o Educational Pipeline," they found[8]:

"Of the 100 Chicana and Chicano students who start at the elementary level, 54 of them drop out (or are pushed out) of high school and 46 continue on to graduate. Of the 46 who graduate from high school, about 26 continue on toward some form of postsecondary education. Of those 26, approximately 17 enroll in community colleges and nine enroll at four-year institutions. Of those 17 in community colleges, only one will transfer to a four-year institution. Of the 9 Chicana/os attending a four-year college and the 1 community college transfer student, 8 will graduate with a baccalaureate degree. Finally, 2 Chicana/o students will continue on to earn a graduate or professional school degree and less than 1 will receive a doctorate."

Did you catch that? Out of every 100 Chicana and Chicano students that begin elementary school, only 8 will graduate from college. Of these 8, only 2 will go on to earn a graduate or professional school degree. And, quite astoundingly, less than 1 will receive a doctorate in any field.

Sadly, similar statistics can be reported for African Americans. In 2005-2006, only 47% of African American male students graduated from high school.[9] In 2007, only 56% of African American high school graduates went on to attend college, and in that same year the college graduation rate for African Americans was only 42%.

What's happening here?

Although there are significant numbers of Latinos and African Americans who are middle class, many Latinos and African Americans come from low-income communities. As a result, large numbers of students of color are forced to attend inferior--and often segregated--public schools which provide inadequate educational training and opportunities.[10] According to UCLA professor Gary Orfield, inner city schools suffer from unequal funding, unqualified teachers, and weak curriculum. Moreover, they are characterized by inadequate staffing, low numbers of high-achieving students, health and nutritional problems, unstable student populations, single-parent households, and high levels of exposure to crime and gang activity. It is also common for urban schools to be ignored for recruitment by colleges and universities and employers. On the other hand, inner city students are more likely to be recruited to the military. In fact, some urban high schools even make special arrangements with the military to facilitate recruitment into the armed forces. Good enough for cannon fodder, but not good enough for Harvard. As a final critique, Orfield notes that U.S. schools are more segregated today than in the 1950's. In my home state of California, which also happens to be the most diverse state in the nation, this segregation is especially apparently. Half of blacks and Asians, and one quarter of Latino and Native American students, attend segregated schools in the Golden State.

All Christians have an affirmative obligation to care about students from low-income communities and to do something to help bring about change. Matthew 25 teaches that what we do (or do not do) "for the least of these" students we do (or do not do) for Jesus. Jesus appears to us in the "distressing disguise" of urban students. If we overlook them and their struggles, then we are overlooking Him as if He were suffering in our midst.

Contrast the experience of inner city students with the experience of students from wealthy families in suburban areas. They are able to enroll in high quality public elementary, junior high, and high schools which prepare them well to compete in the university admissions process. Suburban schools offer rigorous curriculum, numerous honors and advanced placement courses, strong counseling services, and various leadership and service opportunities. Wealthy students are also able to afford fancy, expensive SAT/ACT prep courses which help them get high scores and gain admission to elite universities. In fact, some students begin to study for the SAT in junior high! Such students also often come from "legacies" in which parents and grandparents have attended the same university for generations. All of these factors serve as "plus factors" for suburban students when time comes to apply for college.

In the spirit of the Scripture passage which opened this chapter, educational affirmative action seeks to "level the playing field" for students from low-income communities: "Our desire is not that others might be relieved (in this case inner city students) while you are hard pressed (suburban parents and their children), but that there might be equality (between poor and affluent students alike)." 2 Corinthians 8:13 (NIV).

University affirmative action policies take into account the fact that educational inequity is still an ugly reality in the United States. As a result, urban students are penalized in the admissions process for many reasons which are outside of their control. Every single expression of educational inequality which we have discussed in this chapter (and there are many, many more) has real life consequences in the lives of Students of Color. It's not an abstract discussion for them as it may be for some people reading this book. My past eight years as a professor of Chicana/o Studies has taught me this. Most of my students come from urban backgrounds and they have beat all the odds and struggled to overcome the very educational inequalities we've been discussing. They inspire me every day. It's the greatest privilege not only to teach them, but also to learn from them and to hear their stories.

Most standard admissions criteria work against urban students and students of color for reasons which are outside of their control. This standard criteria includes: grade point average, standardized test scores, high school quality, curriculum strength, geography, alumni relationships/"legacy", and leadership. At first blush you might be tempted to say that these measurements are fair and that they do not penalize inner city kids. Let me break this down, and show how these factors disadvantage urban students in the admissions process.

First off—grades. This seems like a neutral criterion right? Wrong. Elite public schools offer a wide selection of honors and AP courses; inner city schools do not. This means that suburban students have the potential of earning a highly inflated g.p.a. because they get extra points credited to their g.p.a. for every honors course. If they get an "A" in a biology or history honors course then they get 5 out of 4 points on a 4 point scale. If they get a "B" in physics or Spanish, then they still get 4 out of 4 points on a 4 point scale. As a result, many of the most competitive suburban students graduate from high school with g.p.a.'s which exceed 4.4. Contrast that with the experience of urban kids. Since their schools have less funding and less rigorous curriculum, they might be lucky to have a few honors or A.P. classes available for them to take. As a consequence, even if they got just a couple of B's and the rest straight A's, it might only be possible for them to graduate with a 4.0 g.p.a. Is that fair that they've done all that was possible for them to do, and yet they still are put at a disadvantage vis-à-vis their suburban counterparts? 4.4 vs. 4.0? Hmm...

Let's turn next to SAT test scores. The highest predictor of success on the SAT is, guess what—parent income. Why? Because rich parents can pay for their kids to take fancy prep courses and get lots of private tutoring for the SAT and the parents of inner city kids cannot. I did a little research on the pricing for SAT classes and this is what I found:

The most elite "private tutoring" offered by Princeton Review starts at $2,760 "depending on location." "Small Group Instruction," next on the list of fancy courses, starts at $1,499. An "Ultimate Course" is their "most intense" classroom option, and it comes with a 150-point guaranteed score increase. "Depending on location," the Ultimate Course starts at $999. I also recently learned of private SAT tutoring and college counseling "package deals" which range from $5,000 to $15,000!

It is impossible for most urban students to pay for these types of prep courses. Many urban students work 20-30 hours a week at minimum wage jobs just to help their parents make rent and put food on the table. When they come home late at night from their job to study, they're lucky if they can find a quiet space in a closet to get their homework done (this actually happened to one of my students who went on to become a Gates Millenium Scholar). And you expect them to pay $1500 or more for an SAT prep course which is located 10 miles across town? This amount is probably more than their family's rent for a month! Urban students should not be penalized for lower SAT scores because they were not able to afford a $1,000 prep course; they needed the $1,000 to help their families eat and not be homeless.

And then there's "high school quality" and "curriculum strength." As we've already discussed, most inner city schools are poorly funded. This translates into less qualified teachers and a small selection of honors and advanced placement courses. Should an inner city kid get "dinged" in the application process because they attended the only local public school which was available to them and this school happened to be underfunded, understaffed, and offered a weak curriculum?

Alumni relationships and "legacy": Some elite colleges and universities give special consideration to students whose parents graduated from the same school to which a student is applying. If someone's daddy went to Harvard or an Ivy League school, then that Ivy League school will give special consideration to that student's application—not because of anything meritorious on that student's part, but just because their daddy went there 25 years before. Contrast this with the experience of most inner city students who are first-generation college students. They're lucky if they are the first in their family to make it past the 10th grade, let alone have a parent who graduated from Harvard. And so, the "legacy" criterion obviously works against urban students for reasons which are outside of their control.

How about "leadership"? This also seems like one of those factors that is neutral, right? In some cases yes, but in many cases no. If you come from a low-income community and your parents earn a decent living, you might have some time to get active in the "key club," join band, etc. But what about those many urban high school students who have to work 20-30 hours a week at Ralphs so that their family can have food to eat? It is likely that such a student is not going to have much "free time" to devote to running for study body president or president of the Key Club. As a consequence, the high-achieving inner city student with lots of educational potential gets penalized when applying to highly competitive colleges and universities.

About the only factor that does not work against urban kids is "geography." Many universities like to have a geographic mix of students in order to have a diverse student body. Also, public universities also strive to accept a representative sampling of students from different geographic regions in their state. At least urban students are not usually penalized by this.

Affirmative action recognizes that traditional admissions criteria penalize inner city students for reasons which are outside of their control, and seeks to create equality in the university admissions process. The desire is not that suburban students be "hard pressed" when it comes to the university application process, "but that there might be equality" between poor and affluent students alike. Affirmative action seeks to level the admissions playing field for urban students by allowing them to compensate for these various factors which are outside of their control. Did an urban student have a lower SAT score because they did not have $1,000 to shelve out for a fancy prep course? Did an urban student have less opportunities to participate in public service because they had to work at Ralphs for 30 hours a week in the evenings? Was their g.p.a. lower because their high school did not offer many honors courses? Instead of penalizing them for these factors which they had no control over, affirmative action programs assign admissions "points" for non-traditional categories such as "overcoming socio-economic hardship." Rather than "giving a hand-out," affirmative action rewards urban students for working hard, beating the odds, and overcoming tremendous obstacles which their suburban counterparts could not even imagine. Again, the goal is equality.

Affirmative action is justified not only on the grounds of promoting equality of opportunity, but also because educational diversity improves learning outcomes, shatters stereotypes, and prepares students for participation in an increasingly globalized society. When students (or anyone for that matter) get a chance to interact with others who are different from themselves, they get to hear new perspectives. In turn, classroom discussions become livelier and more spirited and interesting. As students interact, they get to form cross-cultural friendships, and as they get to know one another better, racist stereotypes fall by the wayside. As they form new friendships, moreover, they learn that not everyone sees or does things the same way, and this better prepares them for the global workforce of the 21st century.

Those of you who are familiar with constitutional law have already caught on to the fact that I have just described the "diversity rationale" of the United States Supreme Court. I just quoted, almost word for word, the diversity rationale articulated by the Supreme Court in the 2003 affirmative action case of *Gratz v. Bollinger*.[11]  In *Gratz* and its companion case of *Grutter v. Bollinger*,[12] the U.S. Supreme Court held that race-based affirmative action is constitutionally permissible because educational diversity is a "compelling interest." In the words of the esteemed court (which I often find myself in disagreement with):

"Today we endorse... [the} view that student body diversity is a compelling state interest that can justify the use of race in university admissions....[T]he Equal Protection Clause does not prohibit the Law School's narrowly tailored use of race in admissions decisions to further a compelling interest in obtaining the educational benefits that flow from a diverse student body."

"These benefits are substantial. As the District Court emphasized, the Law School's admissions policy promotes "cross-racial understanding," helps to break down racial stereotypes, and "enables [students] to better understand persons of different races." These benefits are "important and laudable," because "classroom discussion is livelier, more spirited, and simply more enlightening and interesting" when the students have "the greatest possible variety of backgrounds."

"In addition to the expert studies and reports entered into evidence at trial, numerous studies show that student body diversity promotes learning outcomes, and 'better prepares students for an increasingly diverse workforce and society, and better prepares them as professionals.'"

What strikes me about the diversity theory articulated by the Supreme Court in the *Gratz* and *Grutter* cases is that it is entirely biblical without even realizing it. This has really struck me in recent years when I've taught about this case in my class, titled, "The History and Politics of Affirmative Action." The Supreme Court's understanding of diversity comports entirely with the "biblical framework of diversity" which we will discuss in great detail in chapters 9-12.

To summarize briefly, here, *every human being holistically reflects the image of God in terms of their individual gifts, talents, personality, cultural background(s), gender, and socio-economic background.* As unique reflections of the image of God, every human being is inherently valuable. They are inherently valuable because they reveal to us an aspect of who God is that we could never understand on our own. Stated another way, we need their God-given diversity in order to learn more about who God is and to have a more well-rounded view of the world.

*Schools, colleges, and universities have a "compelling interest" in maintaining diverse student bodies if they want to partake of, and benefit from, the many educational benefits which flow from the human diversity which God has created.* God made students diverse, and unique reflections of Himself, for a reason. As distinct reflections of the image of God, every student, especially because of their God-given cultural heritage, has a unique contribution to make to the educational system. If we exclude Students of Color from going to school with our sons and daughters, it's us and our children who lose out. If we oppose affirmative action and increased minority representation in colleges and universities, then we turn our backs upon a treasure of blessing which God intends for all students to benefit from. The greater the diversity of our colleges and universities, the more every student stands to profit, because this diversity is a gift from God.

Despite the (hopefully strong) biblical and sociological case I've just made for educational affirmative action, many Christians in America embrace an anti-affirmative action stance. In many cases this perspective is informed by an affiliation with the Republican Party. What's problematic is that they confuse their Republican anti-affirmative action policy stance with their Christian identity. This is a huge problem. Though reasonable Christian minds might differ on the issue of affirmative action, it is wrong for anyone to assert that affirmative action is in any way an "unchristian policy."

*Let me state it for the record: Jesus is not opposed to affirmative action.* In fact, as we looked at in the previous chapter, *He invented it.*

*PraXis*

1. Did you come from an urban high school? Can you identify with the educational inequalities discussed in this chapter? How might God want to use your college education and future profession to help bring change and equality?

2. Did you come from a suburban high school? Were you aware of the vast inequalities of our public educational system prior to reading this chapter? How does it make you feel? How might God want you to use your college education and future profession to help bring change and equality?

# 8  Jesus and the Tea Party: Politics and Christianity

*Christianity is not the same as the political platform of any political party.* God is not a Republican, and He is not a Democrat. He is not a Libertarian and He's not part of the Green Party. He's definitely not a member of the Tea Party.

The conflation of Christianity with partisan politics is one of the scariest things I see whenever I watch CNN, MSNBC, Fox, or any other cable news channel. *Christianity transcends all political parties.* Christians have an important duty to advocate for biblical principles of justice and equity within the political frameworks of their respective countries, but people fall into deep trouble whenever they conflate the Christian message with the agenda of any political party. *The bottom line is that whenever this happens, someone, somewhere, becomes unnecessarily turned off to Christianity because every political party stands for some (even many) policy positions which are opposed to the teachings of Jesus.*

For the veteran, or budding, social activist in the United States, one of the biggest hindrances to coming to know Jesus is the popular conflation of Christianity with the Republican Party. Let me say it loud and clear for the record: *Jesus is not the same as the Republican Party.*

All too many evangelical Christians make the incorrect claim— explicitly or implicitly—that in order to follow Jesus you must also be a Republican. Once again: *Wrong. Wrong. Wrong.*

The Republican Party might stand for some principles which are consistent with the Bible, but it advocates for *many that are not*. Jesus is not opposed to affirmative action, bilingual education, universal healthcare, a living wage, structural changes that will improve our inner city schools, education for undocumented children and college students, or comprehensive immigration reform. In fact, based upon clear biblical support, I have good reasons to believe that Jesus would support some form of each of these policy reform measures.

Unfortunately, many Christians in America fail to do their biblically-mandated due diligence of sifting through political policies using the lens of Scripture. (I am sure that I am guilty of this myself, too; we all have our [many] blindspots) As a consequence, we try to force Jesus into our humanly-constructed political boxes and we end up misrepresenting Christianity to the world. We fail to heed the Apostle Paul's warning in Romans 12: 2 (NIV):

"Do not conform any longer to the pattern of this world, but be transformed by the renewing of your mind. Then you will be able to test and approve what God's will is—his good, pleasing, and perfect will."

By conforming to the "political patterns of this world"--- whether Republican or Democrat, Left, or Right, or whatever—we violate this important biblical principal, and the results are tragic. We end up slapping a Christian label onto every policy position of the political party we belong to. If the Republicans don't believe global warming is true, then we say that that must be the Christian position on the topic. If the Republicans support a particular war in the Middle

East, then we rush to defend that policy decision even if it fails to meet "just war" standards that have been passed down to us by godly Christian theologians like St. Augustine for hundreds of years. If we happen to be on the other side of the political spectrum, we might be tempted to say that a Christian must support abortion as a biblical imperative. At the end of the day, we end up missing God's will on critical social issues—"His good, pleasing, and perfect will."

As previously stated, another consequence of conforming to the political patterns of this world is that it can lead us to misrepresent Jesus. Millions of people then end up rejecting what they think is Christianity but which in reality is just a misguided conflation of Christianity with, for example, the Republican (or more recently, Tea) Party.

One of the things that drives me crazy, for example, is when Christians invoke the memory of Ronald Reagan as if he were a canonized saint. He did some good things, but oh, he did some really bad things which stood in direct opposition to Jesus. For example, did you know that Ronald Reagan fought for racial segregation in housing in California the 1960's? He gained early political notoriety by advocating for Proposition 14. Proposition 14 tragically amended the California state constitution to allow for racial discrimination in housing.[1] It read:

Neither the State nor any subdivision or agency thereof shall deny, limit or abridge, directly or indirectly, the right of any person, who is willing or desires to sell, lease or rent any part or all of his real property, to decline to sell, lease or rent such property to such person or persons as he, in his absolute discretion, chooses. [read: if I want to be racist when I rent or sell a house, then leave me alone]

Proposition 14 was endorsed by conservative groups such as the John Birch Society and the California Republican Assembly. What's worse, this constitutional amendment explicitly overturned The Rumford Fair Housing Act of 1963 which was sponsored by African-American state legislator William Byron Rumford, and which outlawed racial discrimination in housing in California. Yes, Ronald Reagan and the Republican Party in California successfully overturned civil rights legislation barring racial segregation in housing. How do you think it makes me feel when conservative Christians equate Ronald Reagan and the Republican Party with Christianity? It makes me want to scream and say, "Do you want me and my family to be segregated again?"

As governor, Ronald Reagan also opposed César Chávez and the United Farm Workers movement.[2] Yes, he stood against the biblical mandate of economic justice for agricultural workers. This mandate is clearly expressed in the Book of James (5:1-6 NIV):

"Now listen, you rich people, weep and wail because of the misery that is coming on you. Your wealth has rotted, and moths have eaten your clothes. Your gold and silver are corroded. Their corrosion will testify against you and eat your flesh like fire (yes, this is the brother of Jesus speaking!). You have hoarded wealth in the last days. *Look! The wages you failed to pay the workers who mowed your fields are crying out against you. The cries of the harvesters have reached the ears of the Lord Almighty.* You have lived on earth in luxury and self-indulgence. You have fattened yourself in the day of slaughter. You have condemned and murdered innocent one, who was not opposing you."

As a professor who teaches in the UCLA *César E. Chávez* Department of Chicana/o Studies, how do you think it makes me feel when some Christians put Ronald Reagan on a pedestal? It makes me want to throw up.

One more Ronald Reagan example. Remember Bishop Oscar Romero from the previous chapter? The Reagan administration supported the same military leaders, with money and weapons, who probably murdered Bishop Romero.[3] And when thousands of Salvadoran refugees fled to the United States because their family members and friends were being killed by this same oppressive regime, the Reagan administration denied many of their asylum claims and sent them back to Central America knowing that they might be killed.[4]

And so, Ronald Reagan did horrible things which stood opposed to the central Christian values of justice, compassion, and equality. Whenever Christians equate Ronald Reagan with the "golden years" of the 1980's and say we need a leader like him again, my response is: Ronald Reagan is not the same as Christianity, and those were not golden years for everybody.

I'm not alone in feeling this way. Many African Americans and civil rights activists feel the same way, too. According to Professor Ronald W. Walters of the University of Maryland: "Ronald Reagan, it is fair to say, was really an anathema to the entire civil rights community and the civil rights agenda."[5] Reagan was noted for attacking social welfare programs as well as affirmative action programs designed to remedy hundreds of years of racism. He also sought to limit the civil rights protections of the Voting Rights Act and the reach of the U.S. Commission on Civil Rights. The Citizens Commission on Civil Rights was formed to counter the reversal of civil rights progress caused by his administration. In the Commission's own words: "[Reagan caused] an across-the-board breakdown in the machinery constructed by six previous administrations to protect civil rights."[6]

In a famous Supreme Court case called *United States v. Paradise* (1987), the Ronald Reagan administration even intervened on behalf of the Alabama Department of Public Safety which had systematically excluded African Americans from employment and promotion for more than 50 years![7] In fact, the discrimination of the Alabama Department of Public Safety was so thorough that it failed to hire even a single black trooper in the first 37 years of its existence! For this reason and many others, many Christians of color are not big fans of Ronald Reagan. And so, can you imagine how it makes us feel when Ronald Reagan is invoked by some Christians as some sort of modern-day saint?

One final note on President Reagan. He did pass the last amnesty for undocumented immigrants in 1986 through the Immigration Reform and Control Act. I will give him big props for that. I only wish that more Republicans would invoke this part of his legacy, too, and pass Comprehensive Immigration Reform in our present day.

Many evangelical Christians also do a great disservice to the reputation of Christianity in America by uncritically appropriating far-right Republican rhetoric against President Barack Obama. Many evangelical Christians oppose President Obama with as much ferocity as they approve of Ronald Reagan. Let me clarify. They are entitled to their criticisms of Obama. Obama is definitely not perfect and a number of his views do not line up with biblical Christianity. As we've repeated over and over again, Christianity is not the same as the Republican or Democratic Party. That being said, followers of Jesus have the ethical responsibility to not spread unfounded gossip about anyone, and especially the President, to whom, according to Romans 13 we are obligated to show a proper modicum of respect. For example, I have been so upset to read emails circulated by Christians which question the U.S.-citizenship of Barack Obama. As a matter of fact, he has produced the official documentation which establishes his birth in the state of Hawaii. That's it. To continue to insist that he has not is simply factually incorrect and it makes Christians look incredibly ignorant—and racist. If he was blond and from Iowa, would his citizenship be questioned in the same way? I am deeply saddened that some Christians have fallen into the trap of fearing and slandering someone just because he is racially different from them and holds certain views with which they do not agree. It's one thing to disagree with his views; it's quite another to be racist—especially as a follower of Christ.

Sadly, many evangelical Christians have exercised similar misjudgment by insisting that President Obama is a Muslim. If he was a Muslim, fine. We live in a country that respects the religious beliefs of different people and which, by design, does not endorse a specific state religion. But, he's not a Muslim! How many times does he have to say it! I even saw an email circulated by someone who called Obama a Muslim because he changed the White House drapes to a supposedly Middle Eastern-looking design! How ridiculous! Muslim drapes! Come on now.

After reading his memoir I don't think that President Obama has a stellar Christian theological background, in fact, probably quite the opposite. But, at the same time he has clearly, and I believe sincerely, expressed a belief in Jesus. Do these same evangelical Christians subject white luke-warm Christians to such unfair scrutiny? Newt Gingrich has been married three times as opposed to Barack Obama's one-time, and he's changed his theological communion over the years from Protestant to Catholic. I don't hear his faith slandered incessantly. In fact, I distinctly remember Gingrich appearing on a 4th of July television church service of a well-respected evangelical minister a number of years ago. I was deeply troubled because Republican icon Newt Gingrich was being equated with Christianity.

What my fellow Christians do not realize is that they come across as racist every time they publically question the faith of Barack Obama. The message they send is: "Barack Obama has a funny sounding Arabic name (even though Arabic is a cousin language to Hebrew), he's different from us (even though Christianity originated in the Middle East, not in Europe), he has different views from us, and so he must not be a Christian. The implicit message is: we can't trust the sincerity of Obama's faith because he's not white. And that goes to reinforce the stereotype that I've been fighting in every page of this book: that Christianity is a racist religion for white males.

*Christianity and the Libertarian Movement*

In addition to the conflation of Christianity with the Republican Party, it has become increasingly common to encounter Christians who closely identify with the Libertarian movement of Ron Paul. This is disturbing too, and the same principle holds true that I've been stating all along. God is not the same as Ron Paul or the Libertarian Party and the truths of Christianity are not the same as the Libertarian political platform. Libertarians might have some unique and legitimate insights into political issues of the day, but it is very dangerous to equate Libertarian ideology with Christianity—or Ron, or Rand, Paul with Jesus. In embracing the Libertarian Party, many Christians have also, perhaps unknowingly, become adherents of an utterly unbiblical philosophy known as Objectivism.

Objectivism was developed by an atheist Russian-American philosopher and writer named Ayn Rand.[8] She is famous for writing two books—*The Fountainhead* and *Atlas Shrugged*. Objectivism's notion of ethics stands in powerful contradiction to the biblical command to love one's neighbor. When Christians equate Libertarian philosophy with the teachings of Jesus, the results are disastrous, and Christianity once again gets misrepresented to millions of people.

For example, what is the Bible's response to the following questions, as opposed to Ayn Rand's:

1. What is our proper response to God?

*Jesus*: "'Love the Lord your God with all your heart and with all your soul and with all your mind.' This is the first and greatest commandment. Matthew 22: 37-38 (NIV).

*Ayn Rand*: God does not exist.

2. What responsibility do we as human beings have towards one another:

*Jesus*: "And the second is like it: 'Love your neighbor as yourself.' All the Law and the Prophets hang on these two commandments." Matthew 22: 39-40 (NIV). "Anyone who wants to be first, he must be the very last, and the servant of all." Mark 9: 35 (NIV)

*Ayn Rand*: "Man—every man—is an end in himself, not a means to the ends of others; he must live for his own sake, neither sacrificing himself to others nor sacrificing others to himself; he must work for his rational self-interest, with the achievement of his own happiness as the highest moral purpose of his life."

And so, Ayn Rand's teaching on ethical objectivism stands in dire contradiction to the teachings of Jesus. For Jesus, we love our neighbor as an outflow of our love for God. If we love God with all of our being, then we will love our neighbor as our self. Following the example of Jesus, we love our neighbor as our self by putting our neighbor's interests above our own—by being a servant to all. In Ayn Rand's perspective, this is foolishness. For her, "every man—is an end in himself...he must live for his own sake....with the achievement of his own happiness as the highest moral purpose of his life."

It is impossible to follow Ayn Rand's teaching on ethics and be a follower of Jesus. When we try to follow both Ayn Rand and Jesus, we fall off a cliff.[9] And we destroy our Christian witness to the world.

To close, it's important to highlight that Christianity is not the same as the political Left either. I have found supporters of the biblical message of social justice both on the Right and the Left. I have found virulent critics on both sides, too. Some of my most vocal critics, however, have been those on the Left. In fact, I have been quite surprised by the opposition I have received even though I am passionately concerned about issues of justice, race, and gender equity. What I've found is that some people on the Left do not like me because I'm half Chinese. Others don't like me because my wife is white. And, some people on the left especially do not like me because I'm a Christian. Even though one of the loudest rallying cries of the Left is "diversity," I've found that I am offensive because of the diversity which I embody. Apparently I'm not the right kind. This has been a painful experience for me. Quite painful in fact. But, this experience has only served to reinforce what I knew in my head but now know in my heart. Christianity is not the same as the Right or the Left.

*Praxis*

106

1.     Have you, or someone you know, been turned off to Christianity because of how it was confused with Republican politics? Can you think of specific examples from the media?

2.     Have you, or someone you know, been criticized by someone on the political Right or Left, because of your biblical concern for Jesus and racial equality? Read John 15: 18-25. Are you comforted?

# 9   "*Chino-Chicano*": A Biblical Framework for Diversity

*I'm a "Chino-Chicano."*

I was born in East Los Angeles and raised in the small town of Hacienda Heights. My dad is an immigrant from Chihuahua, Mexico and my mom an immigrant from Hubei in central China. The Romeros lost their family fortune during the Mexican Revolution by siding with Pancho Villa, and eventually immigrated to El Paso, Texas. They moved to East Los Angeles in the 1950's and we've been here in Southern California ever since. My mom's family immigrated to Los Angeles from China via Hong Kong and Singapore in the 1950's. My maternal grandfather, Calvin Chao, was a famous pastor in China who launched the first Chinese branch of InterVarsity Christian Fellowship. The Chaos fled their native land because my grandfather was on a communist "hit list." As an interesting side note, my Mom's family traces directly back to the founding emperor of the Song Dynasty!

Growing up "mixed," I had a lot of struggles with racial identity. I was very proud of my Mexican heritage, but at a young age got sent the message that being Chinese was a bad thing. On the first day of first grade a kid walked up to me, pretended to hold an imaginary refrigerator in his hands, and said, "Here's a refrigerator, open it up. Here's a coke, drink it. Me Chinese, me play joke, me do pee-pee in your Coke." Kids are so mean. I was so scarred by that event that I denied my Chinese heritage for the next 18 years. Once I even remember telling a friend that my mom was our housekeeper because I was embarrassed that she came to pick me up from school.

To make matters worse, Hacienda Heights, or at least the school I attended for elementary school during the 1970's and early 80's, was mostly white. (Ironically, today Hacienda Heights is basically half-Mexican and half-Chinese. If I grew up there today I would fit in perfectly. Some friends tease me and tell me I should run for mayor there—I'd win by a landslide based on my racial background alone). As a result, I also wrestled with other types of self-hatred and a deep desire to fit in with my blond peers. Not only did I not want to be Chinese, but I did not want to be Mexican as well. I can remember being called a "beaner" and feeling like I did not fit in because I was not white. In fact, I can distinctly recall two blond kids playing with one another (while I stood alone) and saying to myself, "She's playing with him because they both have yellow hair, and I don't."

These racial identity struggles followed me into my adulthood, and they are, in part, what have driven me so close to God over the years. I've often asked myself: Am I Mexican? Am I Chinese? Am I American? Where do I fit in? I love spending time with my Mexican family and friends, but yet I feel incomplete if I do not also spend meaningful time with my Chinese family and immersing myself in Chinese culture. When I'm with Latinos I'm usually accepted as one of them because I "look Mexican" and can usually "pass." Many people have walked up to me on the street and started speaking Spanish because I am tall with dark wavy hair and tan skin and I can grow a pretty good beard.

Although I look Mexican to many people, I definitely get categorized in other ways as well: Are you "Filipino"? Are you Hawaiian? Are you Middle Eastern? Are you "Chinese with a tan"? Although I don't usually mind being categorized in these ways, as any mixed race person will tell you, it's sometimes painful to be labeled something that you're not.

I can really identify with the following poem, called "Clueless," by my friend, ASU Chicana/o Studies professor Rudy Guevarra.[1] Guevarra is a fellow "Asian-Latino," and his poem captures the frustrations that we as mixed race individuals often feel as a result of being misunderstood and mislabeled. He is a "Mexipino" (Mexican-Filipino) from San Diego, California.

"What's it like to be me you ask?
better yet,
what are you?
so many times
I hear this phrase
from those who don't know
what I am...
I am your illusion, your reality,
your future...
Mestizo you call me,
but what the hell is that?
does that include all of me?
my Asian, Indian, African, and Spanish roots?
can you see my multidimensional character?
the complexity of my being,
my existence
which thrives on the ignorance of the masses
I am the Filipino you once despised
the one you hated,

the Mexican you abhorred, ignore,
and continue to attack
but wait
what if I was both?
could you deal with the double reality
of my presence...
I may be foreign to you,
exotic
even threatening
but so many times
I can be invisible too
my illusion masks my inner thoughts
but not what I see
and it sure as hell won't cloud my sanity
I know who I am
see my genetic, cultural, social,
and political identity
is often in question
but it's all the same to me..."


*Mixed-Race in the Bible*

As an expression of my multiracial struggles, I used to wrestle a lot
with the issue of marriage. I used to say to myself: "If I marry
someone who's Mexican, then my kids will be 75% Mexican. They'll
have a solidified racial identity. If I marry someone who is Chinese,
then they'll be 75% Chinese, probably look mostly Asian, and then
they might have some identity problems. If I marry someone who's
Anglo, then my kids will probably look Latino, even though they'll be
only 25% Mexican. But they'll have the last name Romero, so they'll
probably just pass as Latino." I can't believe I used to think this way!

In my heart I knew that this was not the right way to be
thinking about marriage. Every time I went down this path of

reasoning I would end up deeply frustrated, practically to the point of tears. This led me, one day in law school, to cry out to God and say, "God, please help me to understand the topic of race from Your perspective!" The answer to that prayer is what I hope to share with you in the next several chapters.

After many years of wrestling with my mixed race identity, I feel that God has given me peace, healing, and a deep security in my unique identity. I have discovered a biblically-grounded understanding of race and ethnicity which allows me to be a whole-human being, and which allows me to understand, celebrate, and accept all of who I am. Thank You God. I hope that I might be able to share this understanding with you now, and that what I share might help bring healing to many individuals who have gone through, or are going through, the same struggles I have experienced as a mixed race individual.

As part of my journey of coming to understand my mixed race identity, I have come to learn that I am not alone. According to the 2010 census, there are nearly 7 million mixed race individuals in the United States.[2] My home state of California has a mixed race population of 1.6 million. By 2050, moreover, it is projected that 1 in 5 people in the U.S. population, will be mixed![3] I'm also not alone as an "Asian-Latino." According to the 2000 Census, there are more than 300,000 Asian-Latinos in The United States and 60,000 in California alone![4] Based upon my own experience and these compelling statistics, I am convinced that a biblical understanding of racial identity is now more important than ever.

Before sharing the biblical framework of race and diversity which has brought me so much peace, it's worth noting that there are many prominent biblical examples of interracial marriage and mixed race individuals! Moses, for example, arguably the most important spiritual leader in all of the Old Testament, was married to a Midianite named Zipporah (Exodus 2:21-22). Their first-born son was mixed-race and his name was Gershom. We are later told in the book of Numbers, chapter 12:1-2 (NIV), that Moses' siblings Aaron and Miriam criticized him because of his interracial marriage and used this as a basis to question his spiritual authority:

Miriam and Aaron began to talk against Moses because of his Cushite wife, for he had married a Cushite. 2 "Has the LORD spoken only through Moses?" they asked. "Hasn't he also spoken through us?" And the LORD heard this.

Bible commentators give several explanations for this passage. According to one interpretation, it is said that in calling Zipporah a "Cushite" (or in other translations, "Ethiopian"), Aaron and Miriam may have been taking a racist jab at her for being dark-skinned. They also could simply have been being racist against her because she was not an Israelite. In any event, the Bible is clear that God "heard this" and that he severely punished Aaron and Miriam for their spiritual disobedience and their racist slight (12: 9-13, NIV):

"The anger of the LORD burned against them, and he left them.

10 When the cloud lifted from above the tent, Miriam's skin was leprous[a]—it became as white as snow. Aaron turned toward her and saw that she had a defiling skin disease, 11 and he said to Moses, "Please, my lord, I ask you not to hold against us the sin we have so foolishly committed. 12 Do not let her be like a stillborn infant coming from its mother's womb with its flesh half eaten away."

13 So Moses cried out to the LORD, "Please, God, heal her!"

And so there were serious consequences for being racist against Moses for his interracial marriage—"the anger of the LORD burned against them," and Miriam was struck with leprosy. Apparently England and the United States didn't read this passage too closely when they allowed anti-intermarriage "miscegenation laws" to exist in North America from the 17th century until 1967.

In addition to Moses, Zipporah, and Gershom, other prominent interracial families include Joseph, Asenath, Ephraim and Manasseh; Judah, Tamar, and Perez; Salmon and Rahab; and, Boaz, Ruth, and Obed. Like Moses, Joseph is one of the giants of the Old Testament and one of the biggest heroes of the book of Genesis. He married the Egyptian Asenath who was the daughter of Potiphera, priest of On. Their sons, Ephraim and Manasseh were adopted by Israel as sons entitled to special inheritance in the Promised Land. Through a series of messy human events that's too complicated to explain here, Joseph's brother Judah had a son named Perez with his Canaanite daughter-in-law Tamar! Judah and Perez play important parts in the genealogy of Jesus.

Speaking of Canaanites, Rahab was the famous Canaanite prostitute who protected the spies before the Israelites conquered Jericho. Rahab married a prominent Israelite named Salmon, and they had a son named Boaz. Boaz married—yes, you may have guessed it– Ruth the Moabitess. Ruth has a whole book named after her in the Bible. She is considered a heroine of the faith because she selflessly followed her mother-in-law Naomi back to Bethlehem after her husband Mahlon died, and in those days that was basically like resigning oneself to a life of poverty and alienation. Because of her extreme faith and fidelity, Ruth attracted the favor of Boaz and became his wife. Their son Obed was the grandfather of King David, the "man after God's own heart" and the most famous king in all of the Old Testament. And, the Davidic line traces directly to Mary and Joseph and JESUS! And so, Jesus, the King of Kings has at least four "Gentile" women and several generations of mixed race heritage in his genealogy.

As a mixed race individual, I feel like I'm in good company!

*A Biblical Framework For Diversity*
Now with that mixed-race biblical meandering aside, on to the truth that has set me free. Even if you are not a mixed-race individual I think you will find that what I'm about to share meaningful because it provides a biblical framework for understanding "diversity." This

115

biblical model of diversity seeks to address the question: What is God's purpose behind what we call "race," "class," and "gender"?

Here it is: *I am made uniquely in God's image, and I am His child.*

Every individual uniquely reflects the image of God. The Bible teaches that "God created human beings in his own image" (Genesis 1:27, NLT). Every person holistically reflects God's image in terms of his/her: (1) individual personality, gifts, talents (Psalm 139: 13-16); (2) cultural heritage (s) (Revelation 21:26); and (3) gender (Genesis 1:27). In other words, when you look in the mirror you are staring at a beautiful and unique reflection of who God is. This uniqueness encompasses all of who you are—your personality, gifts, and talents; your ethnic background (s), and your gender. Together, these traits make you uniquely you. You are beautiful, special, and unique, unlike anyone that has ever lived or ever will walk this earth. By God's design, you are valuable and uniquely reflect who He is to the world.

One of the most beautiful declarations of our inherent individual value and worth to God is found in Psalm 139: 13-16 (NIV):

"For you created my inmost being; you knit me together in my mother's womb. I praise you because I am fearfully and wonderfully made; your works are wonderful, I know that full well.

My frame was not hidden from you when I was made in the secret place, when I was woven together in the depths of the earth. Your eyes saw my unformed body; all the days ordained for me were written in your book before one of them came to be."

It may come as a surprise to many of us, but our cultural heritage(s) are critical components of the unique reflection of God's image within each of us. By God's design each of us is given a cultural heritage that helps make us who we are. In other words, our ethnic background is not an accident! God gave it to us! In his famous speech to the Greek Areopagus, the Apostle Paul reminds us of this truth: "From one man he made all the nations, that they should inhabit the whole earth; and he marked out their appointed times in history and the boundaries of their lands. God did this so that they would seek him and perhaps reach out for him and find him, though he is not far from any one of us. "(Acts 17:26-27, NIV). And so, it is not an accident that I was born in East L.A. to my Mexican father and Chinese mother. It is not coincidence that I grew up in Hacienda Heights, spent time in the Bay Area, and now live in Los Angeles. This has been exactly determined for me by God. The same is true for every person reading this book. God has given you your unique cultural heritage! Whether you are Chinese, Korean, English, German, Mexican, American, Armenian, African American, Indian, Native American, or any variation of any of these ethnicities, this is exactly how God planned it to be. Your parents might not have realized it when you were conceived, but God has sovereignly determined what ethnicity and nationality he wanted you to be.

Not only has our cultural heritage been given to us by God Himself, but the Bible teaches that our various ethnic cultures are viewed by God as "treasure" which will last forever! The inherent and eternal value of our national cultures is described in Revelation 21: 22-27(NIV):

> "I did not see a temple in the city, because the Lord God Almighty and the Lamb are its temple. The city does not need the sun or the moon to shine on it, for the glory of God gives it light, and the Lamb is its lamp. The nations will walk by its light, and the kings of the earth will bring their splendor into it. On no day will its gates ever be shut, for there will be no night there. <u>The glory and honor of the nations will be brought into it. Nothing impure will ever enter it, nor will anyone who does what is shameful or deceitful, but only those whose names are written in the Lamb's book of life.</u>"

This passage states that the "glory and honor of the nations" will be brought into the New Jerusalem for eternity (According to the Bible, the time will come when all things are made new, and all the evil, pain, and suffering of this world will be wiped away. This is the amazing "good news" of the Bible. When Jesus comes again, He will make everything new!   In the mean time, our job as followers of Jesus is to love God and be His hands and feet to a hurting and broken world, and help to usher in a foretaste of this amazing future in the present. The "New Jerusalem" is one of the names which the Bible gives for God's future world which will be redeemed and restored when Jesus returns).

What is this "glory and honor" that John is speaking of?  It is interesting to note that most evangelical Bible commentaries completely overlook this text.

The word "glory" which is used in this passage can also be translated as "treasure" or "wealth" of the nations.  Surely John is not describing literal currency or national government coffers. I believe that he is talking about the cultural treasure or wealth of the different ethnic groups of the world. This cultural treasure includes food, music, dance, literature, architecture, etc., as well as the unique cultural personalities of the world.

The first category—food, music, dance, etc. is quite obvious. Every ethnic group has its unique food, art, architecture, musical styles, literature, dance, etc. We enjoy this expression of the "glory and honor of the nations" whenever we go to an ethnic restaurant, visit a museum, listen to world music, go to a concert, or travel abroad. We naturally intuit that there is something unique and beautiful about the different cultures of the world, and this is the glory and honor of the nations.

The second category deserves more explanation. Have you ever noticed that different cultural groups possess different personalities? I have experienced this first hand because of my own cross-cultural heritage and because of my cross-cultural marriage. As previously stated, I am of Mexican heritage on my father's side and Chinese on my mother's. My wife is of Midwestern, German-American heritage.

When I attend a family gathering on my father's side of the family, I observe distinct types of humor, ways of relating to one another, attitudes towards life, etc. The same with my mom's family. I have especially noticed this to be true during my past seven years of marriage to my lovely Midwestern wife.

For example, I've noticed that German-Americans tend to be very time-oriented and financially practical. If we are even five minutes late to an event, I can visibly see the anxiety levels of my Midwestern family rise. From a Latino perspective, on the other hand, it is "relationships" which matter much more than being on time for an event. So, if I'm engaged in a deep conversation with someone, it is of a higher cultural value to me to stay in the conversation and be a little bit late to my next engagement rather than cut off a conversation and appear rude.

In Mexican culture it is also appropriate to "lavish" gifts upon loved ones and friends regardless of the cost. This is seen as a way of showing love, respect, and deference. You could say that one of the Mexican "love-languages" is giving. In Midwestern culture, lavish giving can actually be frowned upon as waste. Nice gifts are valued and appreciated of course, but beyond a certain point it becomes culturally inappropriate.

I actually learned this lesson first hand when I met my wife's family for the first time before we were married. I had made the long journey to Indiana for the annual meeting of the Christian Community Development Association and thought that this would provide me with the perfect opportunity to meet my future in-laws. In anticipation of our meeting over lunch, I went to the airport candy shop and bought mounds of expensive Godiva chocolate to give to them. Without thinking about it very much, my Mexican side was coming out. I thought to myself: "I want to make a good impression and I want them to know that I care. I'll be generous and spend lots of money by buying them good chocolate." Erica was a bit uneasy when she found out because she thought that my generosity would be interpreted as "waste" and the absence of frugality. I was shocked! From my cultural vantage point such lavish giving should have made a positive impression and should have been interpreted as warm generosity. (I ended up giving them the chocolates and it turned out fine!)

What I've learned from my different cross-cultural experiences is that every culture—Mexican, Chinese, Taiwanese, Egyptian, German, Midwestern, etc.—uniquely expresses different aspects of God's heart and personality. As exemplified in the lavish giving of Mexican culture, God is very generous and gracious, and sometimes gives us more than we can hope for or imagine (Ephesians 1:7-8, 3:20). No eye has seen, and no ear has heard, what God has prepared for those who love Him and are called according to His purpose (1 Corinthians 2:9). Relationship is also at the core of God's heart. The divine Godhead relates to Himself in a beautiful mystery that we cannot fully comprehend (Matthew 28:19).

At the same time that this is true, I learn much from my Midwestern family about God, too. I joke with my wife that I'm familiar with about 80% of Midwestern culture by virtue of my American heritage. About 20% though is almost completely foreign. This 20% can sometimes make me feel like an immigrant even though I was born in the U.S. and have lived here all my life.

I learn from them the values of industry and frugality (and starting a savings account for your child when he/she is 3 months old!)(Proverbs 6:6-11). I learn about discipline in our personal relationships with God (1 Corinthians 8: 24-27) and about the importance of individual relationship with Him (Revelation 3:20). (The food is also pretty good too—love them cheese balls and pulled pork sandwiches!)

As another example of what I'm trying to convey, I like to use the example of Mambo Cologne by Liz Claiborne. Trying to capitalize upon the J.Lo/Ricky Martin craze of the early 2000's, executives at Liz Claiborne set out to develop a cologne which captured, in a bottle, the "essence" of what it meant to be Latino. They hired researchers to find out what made Latinos unique and what positive cultural qualities they possess. Among other things, their research revealed that Latinos were "spicy," "sexy," and passionate, and that they were also family-centered. Drawing from their research, Liz Claiborne then set out to create a cologne fragrance which expressed these distinctively Latino qualities. The result was the "Mambo" perfume line, "an up-tempo twist of bergamot and zesty lime, Mediterranean herbs and spices [which] raises the pulse and turns up the heat. A festive tandem of French clary sage and thyme is embraced by exotic, masculine floralcy, and an ultra-sensual fusion of cinnamon leaf, cumin and heart of cedarwood."[5] In 2007, Claiborne released a spin-off cologne–MAMBO MIX—which features an added blend of "spicy oriental fragrance." As a Chinese-Mexican, Mambo Mix is perfect for me. Maybe it captures my unique "essence" and can be called the first "Asian-Latino" cologne (ha).

At first glance, the example of Mambo perfume seems silly. How could someone even attempt to capture the essence of what it means to be Latino in a perfume bottle? Also, Liz Claiborne's so-called "research findings" about Latinidad are just a bunch of crazy stereotypes.

Despite the inaccuracy of Liz Claiborne's stereotypes, I believe they are driving at a profound biblical principle about Latinos and about cultural diversity in general. They realize that Latinos, and all ethnic groups of the world, possess distinct cultural "treasure and wealth" according to the biblical principle expressed in Revelation 21: 26-27.

## Distinct Cultural Sin

On the flip side of things, the Bible also teaches that nations not only possess unique "glory and honor," but also distinct cultural sin. This topic is addressed in verse 27 which states: "*Nothing impure will ever enter it* [the New Jerusalem]..."

This truth also comports with my own personal experience and interaction with the various cultures to which I am connected. In my own experience I have seen the unique ways in which my Mexican, Chinese, American, Midwestern, and German-American cultures have become distorted by sin. Each of the cultures of which I am a part has distinct cultural sins or "impurities." This is true of every nation on earth which has ever existed since the Fall. Just as sin infects us as individuals, it also perverts our larger ethnic cultures. These cultural impurities will not enter the New Jerusalem and the ultimate Kingdom of our Father. This truth—that each culture contains distinct ethnic sin is captured by Chicana feminist Gloria Anzaldúa in her famous work, *Borderlands/La Frontera: The New Mestiza*:

> "Though I'll defend my race and culture when they are attacked by non-mexicanos, conosco el malestar de mi cultura. I abhor some of my culture's ways… But I will not glorify those aspects of my culture which have injured me and which have injured me in the name of protecting me."

"Machismo" represents an example of distinct sin flowing from one of my own cultures. Mexican culture has "machismo" and patriarchy, and extreme honor and shame, which can wound and divide families for decades. Speaking of the destructiveness of machismo, Gloria Anzaldúa also says:

> "[Machismo] cripples its women, como burras, our strengths used against us, lowly burras bearing humility with dignity. The ability to serve, claim the males, is our highest virtue. I abhor how my culture makes macho caricatures of its men. No, I do not buy all the myths of the tribe into which I was born.[5]"

Moving onto one of the other cultures I'm connected to by marriage, I can also say that Midwestern culture is sometimes too practical—to the point of violating God's laws for the sake of practicality. Broader American culture is also sometimes so individualistic that it can forget about the importance of community in God's plan for His church. In America, Christianity sometimes becomes "it's all about my personal relationship with God and everybody else can take a hike." Greed, materialism, and cultural arrogance are also fatal sins of U.S. culture.

And so, as a Chinese-Mexican-American, my unique cultural heritage is given to me by God *and an inextricable part of who I am—for now and forever!* Even though some people might try to take this away from me (by insisting that I speak only English or by denying the importance of *my* cultural diversity), I will celebrate and enjoy my unique blend of Chinese-Mexican-American culture from now into eternity! At the same time, my distinct cultures also have peculiar sins which I hope to excise from my life. I have personally experienced the painful consequences of such cultural sins and I don't want my wife and children to have to go through what I did.

*A Colorblind Conclusion*

Because cultural diversity is God's gift to us, *a "colorblind" approach to life is not biblical.* It's better than racism, but it's not biblical. A lot of people use the term colorblind to mean that God does not show favoritism to any ethnic group and that we all are equal. To say that God does not show ethnic favoritism and that we are all equal in His eyes is true, and vitally important (see Acts 10: 34-35), but it's not the same as saying that God, and therefore, we, should not see color. As we've discussed in this chapter, our cultural heritages are a "treasure" from God that make us His unique children and we will celebrate them for all eternity. I'd like to close this section on cultural diversity with a beautiful quotation from the book of Revelation (7:9-10 NIV) which gives us a splendid picture of the "color-sightedness" of God. In this passage, the apostle John describes heaven and the fact that we "carry our color" into eternity:

After this I looked, and there before me was a great multitude that no one could count, from every nation, tribe, people and language, standing before the throne and before the Lamb. They were wearing white robes and were holding palm branches in their hands. 10 And they cried out in a loud voice: "Salvation belongs to our God, who sits on the throne, and to the Lamb."

As we'll see in the next chapter, "colorblindness" overlooks not only God's beautiful cultural diversity but also the structural inequalities which permeate U.S. society because of historical and contemporary racism...

*PraXis*

1.      Have you ever struggled with your racial identity? You are made uniquely in God's image and in Jesus you are His child. Reflect upon the verses in this chapter. Ask God to heal you. He will.

2.      Visit an ethnic enclave in your city. Enjoy and experience the "glory and honor of the nations"!

3.      What is the distinct "glory and honor" of your own culture(s)? Take some time to thank God for your cultural treasure. Take some time to enjoy some of your own unique cultural treasure!

4.      What are some of the distinct cultural sins of your culture? Have you been wounded by any of these sins. Take some time to talk with God and a friend about your hurts.

# 10 Colorblindness, Structural Inequality, and Trayvon Martin

The colorblind approach to race ignores not only the cultural diversity which God Himself created, but also the stubborn racism which continues to pervade U.S. socio-economic and political institutions.

Supporters of "colorblindness" say that racism is behind us. Sure, racism rears its ugly head once in a while in individual encounters between people, but, as a whole, it's a thing of the past. As evidence they say, "see, we elected a black, Kenyan president…" And then, as we looked at in chapter 9, they call him a Muslim, deny his U.S. citizenship, and proceed to tear him to shreds.

The larger narrative of "colorblindness" goes something like this:

"Yes, it's true, our country has an ugly racist past. We enslaved African Americans for hundreds of years and segregated them through Jim Crow laws. That was terrible. But we've learned from our mistakes. We passed important civil rights legislation in the 1960's which put an end to de jure (legal) segregation and racial discrimination in housing, education, and employment. We experimented with "affirmative action" for a few years, but that was a bad idea. It resulted in "reverse discrimination" against whites and did more harm than good. Racism is no longer a real problem in the United States, so let's forget about race in public discourse and social policy. This was the goal of Martin Luther King, Jr.—to judge people based upon the content of their character instead of the color of their skin…

Like Mitt Romney says, 'America is about equal opportunity, not equal results.' If some people remain poor today it's their own ~~Such~~ fault. They need to work harder, and to stop playing the victim and pulling the race card. America doesn't see race anymore." *I doubt he would say that now*

*This colorblind perspective misses the fact that grave structural inequalities—in education, healthcare, politics, and the law-- continue to pervade urban communities of color throughout the United States.*

Although de jure, legal segregation ended some 48 years ago in the U.S., "de facto" racial segregation (racial segregation in fact) is still quite prevalent. Jim Crow segregation produced unequal conditions of housing, education, health care, legal services, etc., which have not gone away despite the official end to segregation in the 1960's. Jim Crow segregation produced segregated neighborhoods, schools, health care systems, etc., which have continued to replicate themselves up to the present day.

Public schools attended by millions of beautiful brown and black children are vastly inferior to those in rich suburban neighborhoods within the same school district. These same children and their families lack access to quality, affordable health care and legal services, and have few parks and safe public spaces in which to play and just be a kid. The majority of Latinos and African Americans in the United States today continue to experience the invidious lingering effects of Jim Crow segregation.

Lest you think I'm just some radical ethnic studies professor and liberation theology pastor, let's take a look at some staggering statistics which bear this out:  2 out of every 3 valid legal claims of the

poor in California is never heard in court because no attorney will take

their case (because they can't afford to pay); stated another way, 2/3 of

the legal services needs of the poor are unmet in this state and it would

require $394 million per year to close this profound "justice gap."[1]

In 2010, 15.1 percent of all people in the United States—more

than 46 million– lived in poverty.[2]   Poverty of any stripe is horrible,

but poverty is disproportionately prevalent among people of color.

That same year, 27.4 percent of African Americans and 26.6 percent of

Latinos lived in poverty, as compared to 9.9 percent of "non-Hispanic

whites."

There's also a huge wealth gap between whites, blacks, and

Latinos.  The average white family has about $632,000 in wealth.  For

African Americans and Latinos, it's $98,000 and $110,000, respectively.

White families also earn, on average, $2 for every $1 earned by African

American and Latino families.[3]   3 : 2   Hit hard

by Covid

With regards to educational access, only 8% of low-income

students—many of whom are African American and Latino—graduate

from college sometime within their lifetime.  This is as compared with

87% of students from affluent communities who graduate from college

by the age of 24.[4]   Out of every 100 Chican@ students who begin

elementary school, only 8 will graduate from college, 2 will go on to

earn a graduate or professional school degree, and less than 1 will earn

a doctorate![5]   Sadly, similar statistics can be reported for African

Americans.   In 2005-2006, only 47% of African American male

students graduated from high school, and in 2007, only 56% of African

2018 Median
All    63,180

American high school graduates went on to attend college. In that same year the college graduation rate for African Americans was only 42%.[6]

As of 2010, close to 50 million people were uninsured in the United States and this translates into 50,000 avoidable deaths each year![7] Imagine all the people in a medium-sized town dying every year because no one in that town has health care. That's what happens each year in the U.S.

According to a 2009 study, 1 in 4 children go without healthcare in our country, and more than 23 million kids go without adequate healthcare in any given year.[8] About 30 percent of Latino and 20 percent of African American children lack a regular source of health care, and brown kids are almost 3 times more likely than white kids to lack sufficient healthcare.[9]

And so, millions of Chican@s, Latin@s, African Americans, and others, are still segregated from equal opportunity in the United States.

I have a challenge for you which I think may clarify the link between historical racism and contemporary inequality. Check out the following website: http://salt.unc.edu/T-RACES/demo/demo.html

This website was put together by researchers at the University of California and the University of North Carolina. You'll be shocked by what you find. It graphically demonstrates how neighborhoods in California and North Carolina were racially segregated in the 1930's and 40's. Did you get there yet?

The "red" areas were segregated areas inhabited predominantly by people of color—African Americans, Latinos, and Asians. Not only were they residentially segregated, but they also had the worst schools and limited access to basic public services like hospitals, parks, swimming pools, etc. If you were Mexican American, there was a good chance that you attended a segregated, and inferior, "Mexican School" in Southern California.[10] On hot summer days, if you were brown or black, you were often restricted as to when you could use the public swimming pools or parks. If you liked the movies, you were forced to sit in segregated sections of the theater. One city I came across (Pasadena) even had segregated hiking![10] If you were Mexican you could only enjoy God's beautiful mountains on a limited basis in Pasadena. Even some mortuaries were segregated. For many African Americans and Latinos, it was literally segregation from the cradle to the grave. This historical racism gave birth to inferior social, political, and economic institutions in urban communities—which have replicated themselves to the present day.

The "green" areas were occupied exclusively by whites and were segregated through the use of restrictive housing covenants—legal agreements in housing deeds which prohibited the sale of homes to non-whites.[11] These areas had the best schools, hospitals, legal services, parks, pools, etc. They still do.

The "blue" areas were one step below green; and the "yellow" areas were one step above red.

Local realtors and brokers of the time described the red areas as undesirable because they were inhabited by Mexicans, Blacks, Japanese, and even "low class Italians." In describing these red areas they said things like: "Subversive racial elements increasing," or, "Shifting to subversive racial elements."

The green areas were considered more desirable because of their racial exclusivity and homogeneity. One description of a green area states: "Racial protection in perpetuity"—i.e., this area will always be "whites-only" because the legal restrictions in place will last forever.

I dare say almost everyone in the United States would agree that this type of racial segregation was terrible. What most people don't realize, however, is that the areas that were "green" 70 years ago are still largely racially segregated today. Think San Marino, north Arcadia, South Pasadena (if you live in L.A.) Few Latinos and African Americans live in these high brow communities, and these cities still have the best public schools, hospitals, restaurants, parks, pools, skate parks, banks, public services, etc. Schools in these areas have the highest API/standardized test scores, the most qualified teachers, and the most AP (advanced placement) courses available. Their graduates go on to top colleges and universities in high numbers, and they become future doctors, lawyers, teachers, engineers, architects, university professors, judges, and senators. Unless you are able to afford the million dollar price tags on the homes, or $5,000 a month rent, you, and your kids, are locked out of these communities.

In fact, if you are a person of color, you may even still experience some racial hostility—passive or aggressive—when you enter some of these communities. After driving into one of these communities a close African American friend of mine was told, "Go back hood!" See also my blog post about the Black family that was recently driven out of the city of Yorba Linda in Orange County[12]: www.jesusforrevolutionaries.org/driven-out-a-black-familys-battle-with-housing-discrimination-in-the-o-c/

The areas that were marked "red" and "yellow" 70 years ago are still largely poor, impoverished, and inhabited largely by people of color. Examples of these communities in L.A. include: East L.A., south Monrovia, parts of Pasadena, Baldwin Park, and El Monte. These formerly red areas still have the lowest performing and most poorly funded schools, and they still lack adequate health care, legal services, parks, pools, banking services, etc. They also lack access to healthy food options ranging from restaurants to affordably-priced fruits and vegetables. What you won't find is a lack of fast food joints and pay-day loan places. You'll also be more opt to find pollution and racist policing practices in these communities as well.

If we take a "color-blind" approach to social policy and wrongly assume that racial disparities no longer exist in the United States, then we will miss all of the–very real– institutional inequality that I've just described. We will also continue to perpetuate a racial underclass for decades to come. A colorblind perspective will produce an upper and middle class which is mostly "white," peppered with some Blacks and Latinos. If we don't get to the root of race-based structural inequality in the United States, then poverty and injustice will continue to replicate itself in our communities of color.

*Racial Fault-Lines: Voting Rights, Immigration Reform, Affirmative Action, and Trayvon Martin*

This color-blind approach has brought us into dangerous racial territory in recent months...

*Voting Rights.* On June 25, 2013, the United States Supreme Court emasculated half of the historic Voting Rights Act. The reasoning of the majority: Racism is not a huge problem in the United States and the South is no longer extremely racist like it used to be. The day after this decision was handed down what happened? Numerous states like Texas re-implemented voting practices and voting districts which disenfranchised thousands of Latinos and African Americans. The result—millions of Latinos and African Americans feel politically ostracized. Remember the original Tea Party: taxation without representation. Very bad.

*Immigration Reform.* Despite wide-scale national support for comprehensive immigration reform, at the time of writing this chapter, Republican members of the U.S. House of Representatives are resisting the passage of compassionate legislation which would provide a pathway to citizenship for 11 million undocumented immigrants. The result—millions of Latinos, including myself, feel racially ostracized.

*Affirmative Action.* On June 24, 2013, the United States Supreme Court in theory upheld the constitutionality of race-based affirmative action in public universities, but at the same time opened up the door to future constitutional challenges by conservative opponents of affirmative action. The result—millions of supporters of affirmative action like myself feel somewhat relieved, but leery of future legal challenges brought by those who embrace a color-blind approach and who think that racism is no longer a problem in the United States.

*Trayvon Martin.* On July 13, 2013, George Zimmerman was acquitted in the murder of Trayvon Martin. He was also acquitted for the lesser charge of manslaughter. 17-year old Trayvon, who had no criminal record, was killed by Zimmerman at 7:15 p.m. while returning home from buying Skittles and a can of iced tea. How does this make me and millions of others of Latinos and African Americans feel? It makes us feel that the lives of black youth in this country apparently don't matter. We were already aware of unequal justice in the American legal system for People of Color, now we are even more persuaded.[13]

*As a result of these recent legal and political developments, millions of People of Color now feel angry, hurt, and alienated. It's a scary place to be. It's the stuff of civil unrest.*

The Christian witness in the United States is on the line. Will the culturally diverse Christian church in America listen to its African American and Latino brothers and sisters about the Trayvon Martin case, immigration reform, and these recent Supreme Court rulings? If the mainstream American suburban church fails to listen, it will rupture its relationship with millions of African American and Latino Christians, and it will destroy its witness to millions of non-Christians in the United States and around the globe.

*In response to all of this heaviness, I can't help but pray. Will you join me?*

Lord, we are living in a critical historical moment. Racial tensions are high, and there is little understanding between those who deny the prevalence of racism and those who are still deeply affected by it. We know that the roots of poverty in our country have deep historical roots which still play themselves out today on a daily basis—both in the lives of individuals and entire communities.

Please bring healing and reconciliation, Lord. Help us to forgive those who trespass against us, just as You have forgiven us in our many imperfections. Teach us to love You more, and to love our enemies. Send us out to be Your ambassadors of reconciliation. We cannot do this on our own. We need You. In Jesus' Name. Amen.

*PraXis*

1.    Do you live in an urban community? Was it historically segregated? Is it the product of "white flight"? Can you see the connection between historical segregation and the current conditions of your community?

2.    Do you live in a suburban community? Was it ever segregated? Do some research into the historical origins of your city. *(yes)*

3.    Go    to    the    following    website: http://www.healthycity.org/

Research the socio-economic demographics of your city. Do you see evidence of structural racism? Talk to God about it. What do you think He would like you to do about it?

2019

Men
Women

# (Hall)
67,123
52,085

Me
57,500
47,300

# 11    Gender

In chapter 9, we introduced a biblical framework for understanding cultural diversity, and in the last chapter, we examined the serious negative consequences of projecting a colorblind perspective upon contemporary U.S. society. We've said that the Bible teaches that "God created human beings in his own image" (Genesis 1:27 NLT), and that every person holistically reflects God's image in terms of his/her: (1) individual personality, gifts, talents (Psalm 139: 13-16); (2) cultural heritage (s) (Revelation 21:26) ; and (3) gender (Genesis 1:27). So far, we've focused upon the cultural dimensions of the image of God. This chapter will continue our thoughts on biblical diversity, but will turn to the important concept of gender.

## "WOMYN" HOLD UP HALF THE SKY

In addition to our cultural heritage, our gender also uniquely factors into the unique reflection of God's image within each of us. Genesis 1: 27 (NLT) states:

> "So God created human beings in his own image.
> In the image of God he created them;
> male and female he created them."

Men and women are equal in the eyes of God, because men and women uniquely reflect the image of God. As a famous Chinese proverb states: "Women hold up half the sky." God made men and women to show the world different aspects of who God is. Men are intended to uniquely reflect God's image in certain ways, and so are women. Neither sex has a monopoly on God or God's image. Men and women need each other so that they can teach other more about who God is. Without women, men will always be limited in their view and perspective of God, and vice-versa.

This is not to say, however, that men and women do not reflect the image of God in similar ways as well. In fact, men and women probably reflect the image of God in more common, rather than distinct ways.

The truth—that men and women uniquely reflect the image of God—has been historically twisted and abused to exclude women from positions of leadership and many professions. The argument of religious sexists was (and sadly, sometimes still is) that women can't take positions of political authority such as president, senator, state legislator, mayor, etc. because they have been created by God to live in quiet subservience, and service to, men. I.e., they don't reflect God in terms of the ability to lead. In fact, I've even heard it said by a major Christian leader that the reason why so few women serve in the United States Senate is because they are not hard-wired for strong, tough leadership positions! (Not being able to vote on a national level until 1920 and exclusion from elected office for hundreds of years of course had nothing to do with it!).

Tragically, a similar line of reasoning has been made by some Christians over the years to limit female professional choices to the domestic sphere. The argument was basically the same: women were made by God with certain gifts and talents and abilities which confined them to domestic roles. As a result, women should be limited to a few career choices—secretary, teacher, and nurse to name a few, and they should definitely not be allowed to take a man's place in higher education. In the 1950's and 60's for example (often cited by some evangelicals as "golden years" in this country), many law schools had official policies which excluded women. Erwin Griswold, of Harvard Law School, for example, stated in 1964: "[T]here could never be a great influx of women into the school...because the policy was never to give any man's place to a woman."[1]

I don't say this to in any way disparage female participation in the professions of teaching or nursing. These are great professions for those who feel a calling to be a part of them. But, it was wrong to exclude women from other professions based upon skewed theology. By the way, I think that the personal decision to be a stay at home mom in order to focus upon the raising of one's family is an amazing calling to have as well! In fact, it's probably the toughest job in the world.

And, just in case you're wondering, this is coming from a guy who changes diapers, does the dishes (most nights), and cleans showers and toilets.

Let me say for the record: *I stand totally opposed to the types of historical abuses previously discussed, and I believe that women possess a God-given equal capacity for leadership and participation in any profession they might choose to pursue.* In fact, I am here to say that the Bible offers many examples of strong, powerful women leaders.

Deborah and Jael offer compelling examples of female leaders in the Bible. In the Book of Judges (chapter 4, verses 4-7, NIV) we are told that Deborah was the President, Supreme Court, and Five-Star General of Israel all rolled up into one! :

> 4 Now Deborah, a prophet, the wife of Lappidoth, was leading Israel at that time. 5 She held court under the Palm of Deborah between Ramah and Bethel in the hill country of Ephraim, and the Israelites went up to her to have their disputes decided. 6 She sent for Barak son of Abinoam from Kedesh in Naphtali and said to him, "The LORD, the God of Israel, commands you: 'Go, take with you ten thousand men of Naphtali and Zebulun and lead them up to Mount Tabor. 7 I will lead Sisera, the commander of Jabin's army, with his chariots and his troops to the Kishon River and give him into your hands.'"

Deborah was in fact so powerful and well respected as a godly leader of Israel that the powerful military leader Barak (a variation of a well known, though sometimes unpopular name these days) refused to go into battle without her!

> "8 Barak said to her, "If you go with me, I will go; but if you don't go with me, I won't go."

This story in Judges gets even better because of another feisty woman named Jael. Let me bring you up to speed. Barak ends up obeying the orders of Deborah and his army destroys the opposing army. One glitch though. Sisera, the general of the enemy's army escapes capture and sneaks away into Jael's tent because of a special alliance that existed between him and Jael's family. Then the story starts to get really good. Jael gives Sisera some milk and a blanket. He falls asleep. Then, we are told (Judges 4: 21-22 NIV):

"But Jael, Heber's wife, picked up a tent peg and a hammer and went quietly to him while he lay fast asleep, exhausted. She drove the peg through his temple into the ground, and he died.

Just then Barak came by in pursuit of Sisera, and Jael went out to meet him. "Come," she said, "I will show you the man you're looking for." So he went in with her, and there lay Sisera with the tent peg through his temple—dead."

What! Did you catch that. She drove a tent peg into his temple and won the entire war! Talk about a strong woman who knows how to handle herself! And so in one single chapter in the book of Judges, these examples of Deborah and Jael totally dispel the myth— and bad theology— that women cannot be political leaders (even presidents), judges, prophets, and warriors. I wonder what Deborah and Jael would have thought about U.S. military policy towards women in combat?

Romans chapter 16 is another overlooked chapter of the Bible that puts a silence to historic Christian biases against women leaders in the church. In verses one and two, Paul (the former persecutor of the Christian movement turned early church leader) states:

"I commend to you our sister Phoebe, a deacon of the church in Cenchreae. 2 I ask you to receive her in the Lord in a way worthy of his people and to give her any help she may need from you, for she has been the benefactor of many people, including me (NIV)."

These verses establish that women are biblically entitled to serve in the leadership role of "deacon" in the church. Some scholars also prefer to translate the Greek word used in this passage as "minister." This ruffles a lot of feathers because it directly implies that women should be allowed to serve as ministers in the church. But the controversy goes even deeper...

In verse 7 Paul tells us:

> 7 Greet Andronicus and Junia, my fellow Jews who have been in prison with me. They are outstanding among the apostles, and they were in Christ before I was.

This verse makes even more people uncomfortable because it is quite likely that the name translated as "Junia," or "Junias" (in other translations,) refers to a woman. And if Junia was a woman, and she was excellent "among the apostles," then she was an "apostle"! Such apostles held one of the highest leadership positions in the early church.[2]

Among those who oppose women holding high ecclesiastical office, there are those who say that the name Junias actually referred to a man, or that "outstanding among the apostles" is better translated as "well known to the apostles." Based upon this perspective, it is said that Junias was a man who was an apostle, or, that Junia was a woman who was well known to the male apostles of the time.

Christians who love Jesus make both arguments about who Junia was and whether or not she/he was an apostle. Strong evidence exists to support the argument that Junia was a woman and that she was an "apostle." I'm not a professionally trained theologian so take my argument as you choose, but I can read Bible commentaries as well as many and I know that a good argument can be made for this position. First, there is almost universal agreement among the church fathers that Junia was a woman. Also, most commentaries share the perspective that Junia was an apostle.

Another biblical basis for female leadership in the church is based upon the doctrine of spiritual gifts (see Romans 12:4-8; 1 Corinthians 12:1-28; Ephesians 4:8, 11-16; Acts 6:1-7; 1 Peter 4:10, 11). The Bible teaches that God gives spiritual gifts to believers in Christ without respect to gender (or race and class for that matter). These gifts include those of teacher, pastor, and prophet. In other words, it doesn't say that only men are given the gifts of teacher, pastor, and prophet. And so, this provides more biblical support for female leadership in the church.

It's not simply an issue of "liberal" vs. "biblical" as some people like to make it out to be. Quite frankly, it drives me crazy when people mischaracterize the issue in this way. There are thousands of Jesus-centered churches which enthusiastically embrace the role of women in leadership and pastoral positions. As followers of Jesus we can respectfully disagree with one another about this issue, but it is not right for anyone to slander another person's biblically grounded viewpoint on the matter.

As someone who was ordained by a legendary female African American inner city pastor, I admit I'm biased. Before her recent passing, God used Pastor Faye Newman in incredible and amazing ways to share His love and teaching with thousands of people. You may never have heard of Pastor Faye Newman, but she was a legend of inner city ministry in South Los Angeles. As Henri Nouwen wrote, the greater part of God's work in this world often goes unnoticed. That's definitely true of Pastor Faye. She may not have been famous in the world's eyes, but she was used by God to touch the lives of hundreds of thousands of individuals in South Central Los Angeles and beyond. Pastor Faye was also a spiritual mother and mentor to me, and I am so proud to say that she was the person that God chose to ordain me to Christian ministry.

Together with Bishop B.J. Luckett, Pastor Faye established a food ministry in South Los Angeles called the Neighborhood Outreach Council. In fulfillment of Matthew 25, the Neighborhood Outreach Council partnered with Here's Life Inner City and 158 churches in South L.A. to feed hundreds of thousands of people. In fact, at its height, the Neighborhood Outreach Council fed 400,000 people per month! As a natural outflow of this profound demonstration of love, hundreds, if not thousands of people came to know Jesus as their personal and loving Savior.

Pastor Faye also had a big heart for African American and Latino youth of South L.A. As a native of South Central and graduate of Jordan High, she lived in South L.A. from 1955 until her passing on June 12, 2012. She lived through the Watts and Rodney King Rebellions, and even heard Rev. Martin Luther King, Jr. preach in her community. She had the highest street "creds." Drawing from her long-standing ties to the community and huge personality, Pastor Faye formed the National Low Riders Association in an effort to bring together the warring factions of Los Angeles gangs and to reach out to the youth of South L.A.

Through their cars, Pastor Faye brought together bloods and crips and other rival gangs, and organized them to feed the homeless and serve the poor! In 2008, she became the "1st lady" (and first female member) of the Individuals Car Club. Pastor Faye also drove and owned two amazing low riders which depicted scenes from the Bible!

I saw God powerfully at work through Pastor Faye as a minister of the gospel. She was a living, breathing example of Deborah, Jael, Phoebe, and Junia all rolled into one! And, I'll admit this biases me towards an interpretation of Romans and other scriptural passages which favors the ordination of women in the church. If I'm wrong, God please show me.

I'd like to close this section with an inspirational quote from Pastor Faye which I think we can all learn from and live by:

> "As I continue to serve God, I continue to pray to the Lord, that He would make me one of His bond slaves, for He has set my feet upon a rock and He planted me there and I thank Him for my salvation, for He has sealed me with His Holy Spirit." Ephesians 1: 13, 14.

## La Virgen de Guadalupe

In the previous section, we examined a biblical framework for gender and highlighted the fact that the Bible features important accounts of powerful and empowered women. I'd like to continue my discussion of gender by talking about the most famous woman of the Bible: Jesus' mom, the Virgin Mary. Like generations of Christians before me, I call her blessed. She is the mother of my Lord, how could I do any less. Together with the physician and gospel writer Luke, I take to heart the truth expressed in the following famous scripture known as the Magnificat (Luke 1:48b-53 NIV):

> "From now on all generations will call me blessed,
> 49 for the Mighty One has done great things for me—
> holy is his name.
> 50 His mercy extends to those who fear him,
> from generation to generation.
> 51 He has performed mighty deeds with his arm;
> he has scattered those who are proud in their inmost thoughts.
> 52 He has brought down rulers from their thrones
> but has lifted up the humble.
> 53 He has filled the hungry with good things
> but has sent the rich away empty.

As a follower of Christ whose family comes from Mexico, I especially take to heart verses 52-53:

> "He has brought down rulers from their thrones but has lifted up the humble. He has filled the hungry with good things but has sent the rich away empty."

As will be discussed in a later chapter, the Spanish maligned the name of Christ by using the Conquest of Mexico as an excuse to pillage and murder millions of people. Within the first hundred years of the Spanish conquest, more than 20 million indigenous people died in central Mexico—90% of the total indigenous population in that area. How could the indigenous peoples of Mexico believe in the God of the Spaniards after the Spaniards had done such horrible things?

This is where the Virgin Mary brings me hope. Under inspiration of the Holy Spirit, the Virgin Mary declares emphatically in these verses that God is upset with arrogant rulers, indeed that He takes them down from their thrones of authority. She states clearly that God is angered by economic injustice and when rich people have lots of food and poor people have none. But she doesn't stop there. She also speaks in the affirmative and declares that God will lift up the humble and fill the hungry with good things. As we used to say in my Spanish-language Latino church growing up, "Amen."

In my view, these biblical truths are embodied by the famous story of the Virgin of Guadalupe. For Catholic and Orthodox readers of this book, this story presents no theological conflict. For Protestants, and especially Mexican Protestants like myself, simply addressing this topic can cause deep theological wrestling and defensiveness. I understand that I'm touching upon a deeply controversial topic, but I think that its impossible for me, as a Mexican and Latino, to write a book about faith and justice and to ignore a discussion of "La Virgen."

Without compromising any of their theological convictions, I hope that my fellow Protestants might consider a new perspective on the story of the Virgin of Guadalupe—one that I've come to after a number of years of reflection: the account of the Virgin of Guadalupe reminds me that God cares about the poor of Mexico and that He did not turn a blind eye to the Spanish Conquest. The Virgin of Guadalupe is a powerful symbol of the fact that God loves the indigenous people of Mexico and will one day bring them justice. In light of that preface, here's the story...

According to tradition, the Virgin Mary, clothed in the appearance of a humble, indigenous Mexican woman, appeared to Juan Diego on December 9, 1531 (Just 10 years after the capture of Mexico City). What follows is an account of the Virgin's appearance which was originally written in Nahuatl (the Aztec language) in 1545. It was composed by Don Antonio Valeriano, an indigenous noble with blood ties to the famous Emperor Moctezuma. Titled "Nican Mopohua," it is considered a masterpiece of the Aztec language[3]:

> "At the beginning of December, a poor Indian named Juan Diego left his house one Saturday morning to attend divine service. On the way, as he passed the hill of Tepeyacac ("Hill of the Nose," in Nahuatl), he was startled by a song coming from the summit. The sweet, tender singing surpassed the trilling of the most exquisite birds. Juan Diego stopped, entranced, and mused, 'Is it my luck to be worthy to hear such music? Is it a dream perhaps? Did I get up from my bed? Where am I? In Paradise, in heaven perhaps? I don't know.'
>
> The singing ceased and a heavenly sweet voice called him from the hill-top, 'Juan, my little one, Juan Diego.' Filled with joy, Juan Diego was not at all frightened, but climbed the hill in search of the mysterious voice.
>
> When he reached the top, he saw a lady who bade him approach. It was a wonderful lady of superhuman beauty. Her raiment shone like the sun; the rock on which she set her foot seemed to be hewn from precious stones and the

ground red like the rainbow. The grass, the trees and the bushes were like emeralds; the foliage, fine turquoise; and the branches flashed like gold..."

Astonished by the appearance of the Virgin, Juan Diego listened as she gave him special orders:

"'I wish a shrine to be built here to show my love to you. I am your merciful mother, thine, and all the dwellers of this earth. To bring to pass what I bid thee, go thou and speak to the bishop of Mexico and say I sent thee to make manifest to him my will...'"

Juan Diego was commanded to request from the Spanish bishop of Mexico that a special church be built which would represent God and the Virgin's love for the indigenous population of Mexico. Juan Diego listened to the Virgin and went several times to speak with the Bishop but he would not believe. Instead, the Bishop demanded a special sign from heaven. Juan Diego also continued to experience apparitions of the Virgin Mary. On one of these occasions it is reported that she helped him to gather beautiful flowers in his cloak. Juan Diego went to see the Bishop one last time and a miracle took place:

"In the bishop's palace he had a long time to wait. The servants, suspecting from his attitude that he was hiding something in his arms, began to bait him. Seeing his refusal to show them what he was carrying, they began to tug at his cloak, in spite of the tearful petitions the poor Indian put up. Terrified the flowers would fall to the floor, he lifted a corner of his cloak to placate his tormentors. But a miracle! the blooms, fresh and fragrant before, to the gaze of the servants seemed as if stuck to Juan Diego's cloak... The Lord Bishop commanded at once that he should be brought before him. Juan Diego prostrated himself before him and said:

'Sir, I have done thy command. I went and told the Lady of Heaven thou wast asking for a sign that thou mightest believe me.' The Indian related what the Holy Mother of God had told him and described the glory in which she had lately appeared to him. Then he unfolded his white cloak and, as the lovely blooms were strewn on the floor, the miraculous image of Our Lady of Guadalupe suddenly appeared on the cloth just as it is to be seen today, painted by a divine hand on the cape of Juan Diego."

Through this story I see that God "broke through" the misrepresentation of the Conquest to the indigenous people of Mexico and revealed to them, that, despite the terrible misrepresentation which was occurring, He loved them. He broke through with Jesus' mom. Regardless of your perspective on the historicity of the Virgin of Guadalupe story, I hope we can agree on one point: the Virgin is a powerful symbol of the fact that God loves the poor of Mexico and he has not overlooked the injustices that they have suffered for the past 500 years.

To conclude the account, the church was built and it is reported that more than 10 million indigenous people came to faith in Christ. Pope John Paul II called Juan Diego the greatest evangelist of all time! You can still visit the church and see Juan Diego's white cloak with the miraculous image of Our Lady of Guadalupe "painted by a divine hand." And, miraculously, the image has not faded.

In sum, there is no room in a biblical framework for sexism or oppressive patriarchy. Men are no better than women, and women are no better than men. Instead, men and women are uniquely beautiful in a complementary fashion. They also share the divine image in many important ways as well. Sadly, men have twisted and dismissed these truths for millennia. The result has been sexism and inequality between the sexes which continues on both an individual and structural level to the present day in the United States, Latin America, and wherever you have men.

*PraXis*

1.     Have you been discouraged from investigating Christianity in the past because you thought it was a sexist religion? How does this chapter change your perspective? Talk to God about your feelings, thoughts, and questions.

2.     Interested in learning more about gender equality from a Christian perspective? Visit the Christians for Biblical Equality website: http://www.cbeinternational.org/

## 12    Class

I did a very "unrevolutionary" thing recently. I spent three nights at a "4 Diamond" hotel in La Jolla. It was actually a gift from my parents to me and my family. I am very grateful for the gift. It was luxurious. And very restful. The service was nice, too...

*why is he complaining*

On one occasion we arrived to our room and our toilet was stuffed. So that night they sent us hummus and two award winning beers to make it up to us. On another night our pay per view didn't work, so they sent us chips and guacamole and a card typed with a personalized apology.

*which paid the valet*

To be honest, by the end of our stay, we were starting to get disgusted by the luxury and pretension of the place. Every time we wanted our car we had to give a tip to the valet which was equivalent to the daily wage received by millions of people in the developing world. There were lots of rich business people and travelers from the United States and Mexico. They were always dressed to the hilt. One morning I wandered down to the coffee shop with my daughter in tow to buy orange juice and two muffins for $50 million dollars. As I looked around, I saw an upper class Mexican family looking like they had just come from Miami out of an episode of "Burn Notice." Whether white, slightly tanned, Asian, or African American, it seemed that many people at the hotel were preoccupied with status, and the money they had or pretended to have. I felt it. To be honest, it was

*Very judgemental*

intoxicating. The luxury made you feel self-important and it fed your ego. It made you want more and more…Pretty scary…

It felt like we were at a temple dedicated to excessive luxury and the worship of the American Dream.

This story provides a good segway into this chapter's discussion of "class" and the image of God.

As we've talked about in the last several chapters, each of us uniquely reflects the image of God in terms of our cultural heritage and gender. *We also reflect the image of God in terms of our natural abilities and talents.* I.e., some of us are artists, some are good at putting things together mechanically, some are good at music, some are good at math, some are good with ideas, some are good with science, some are good at painting, some are good at carpentry, some are good at making logical arguments, etc.

As human beings who have turned our backs on God, we have placed high economic value on some divine giftings and low value upon others. If someone is good at memorization and arguing, then we give them a law license and pay them $100,000 a year. If someone is good at understanding science and memorizing facts about the way the human body functions, then we call them a doctor and pay them $200,000 a year. On the other hand, if someone is good with mechanical things and fixing widgets, then we might pay them $15 an hour and force them to join a union. Along similar lines, if someone has less intellectual prowess and is gifted in manual arts, we might pay them the federal minimum wage and hope that they can come up with enough money to pay their rent and feed their family.

In other words, we have created socio-economic classes based upon divine giftings. We have placed a premium on certain God-given gifts and abilities, and devalued others. From God's perspective, every individual gifting and skill set is equally valuable. The plumber reflects the image of God just as much as the cardiologist, and the sandwich maker at Subway's just as much as the corporate lawyer from Wilson & Sonsini.

In fact, the Bible warns against classism and looking down upon the poor. One of my favorite scriptural passages on this topic is found in the epistle of James:

"Believers in humble circumstances ought to take pride in their high position. But the rich should take pride in their humiliation—since they will pass away like a wild flower. 11 For the sun rises with scorching heat and withers the plant; its blossom falls and its beauty is destroyed. In the same way, the rich will fade away even while they go about their business…" (James 1: 9-11 NIV)

"My brothers and sisters, believers in our glorious Lord Jesus Christ must not show favoritism. 2 Suppose a man comes into your meeting wearing a gold ring and fine clothes, and a poor man in filthy old clothes also comes in. 3 If you show special attention to the man wearing fine clothes and say, 'Here's a good seat for you,' but say to the poor man, 'You stand there' or 'Sit on the floor by my feet,' 4 have you not discriminated among yourselves and become judges with evil thoughts?

'Listen, my dear brothers and sisters: Has not God chosen those who are poor in the eyes of the world to be rich in faith and to inherit the kingdom he promised those who love him? 6 But you have dishonored the poor. Is it not the rich who are exploiting you? Are they not the ones who are dragging you into court? 7 Are they not the ones who are blaspheming the noble name of him to whom you belong?" (James 2: 1-7 NIV)

As the result of forgetting this biblical truth that all are equal in the image of God based upon their skill sets, human beings have created classism. The rich man in the Polo shirt who walks around with a fancy cell phone looks down upon the undocumented worker who makes his hamburger at Burger King for $5.00 an hour. The pastor of a "mega church" calls in security to kick out a homeless man who walks into the sanctuary. The severely surgically altered woman at Fashion Island in Newport Beach who carries a poodle in her purse shuns the stinky plumber who de-clogs the copper pipes of her gated-community home. The rich denounce the poor for being lazy and decry all government assistance programs. The upper middle class pass Proposition 209 in California and denounce race-based affirmative action programs as unnecessary despite the deplorable discrepancies between a public school education in the suburbs and one in "the hood." They block efforts to reform health care so that all people can have access to decent doctors and hospitals. And so, the poor, over the millennia, like most women, have been despised and shunned.

*making 50/w*

*Not all*

*Praxis*

1.      Read more about the problem of homelessness and volunteer or donate to make a difference. The following website from the Union Rescue Mission is a great place to start: http://urm.org/

2.      I recently heard of a pastor who called security on a homeless person who entered his church. This made me sick. The next time a homeless person enters your church, talk to them and make them feel welcome.

Lots of judgement
Lots of mixing class w/ income
There is class judgement
There is income disparity
The 2 are not the same
Homelessness less about class than it is about income dispar[ity]
mental illness, addiction
and (for some) choice.

## 13    Summing Up the Image of God: Neither Jew nor Gentile, Male nor Female, Slave nor Free

What I have tried to communicate in chapters 9-12 is that biblical Christianity, despite all of the historical misrepresentations to the contrary, stands for the proposition that every individual human being is equal and has intrinsic value in the eyes of God. *Every human being uniquely reflects the image of God in term of their individual personality, gifts and talents, cultural backgrounds, and gender.*    In the words of Paul:

> "So in Christ Jesus you are all children of God through faith, for all of you who were baptized into Christ have clothed yourselves with Christ.  There is neither Jew nor Gentile, neither slave nor free, nor is there male and female, for you are all one in Christ Jesus. (Galatians 3:26-28 NIV)

Biblical Christianity transcends race, class, and gender.   Paul's words were shocking to the ears of his first-century hearers.    He announced clearly and without apology that God accepts all who come to Him by faith in Jesus, regardless of their:  (1) ethnic background— "there is neither Jew nor Gentile"; (2) socio-economic standing— "neither slave nor free";   (3) or gender—"nor is there male and female."  All are equal in the eyes of God.  *There is no biblical basis for racism, classism, or sexism.*

On the contrary, our ethnic backgrounds, gender, and individual giftings and talents (which correspond to class in society), find their ultimate expression and fulfillment in Christ. We are made in His image, and in Him are children of God. As we follow Him and are made more and more like Him, He transforms us into the individuals that He made us to be. He makes our cultural ancestries— our cultural glory and honor-- to shine, while at the same time revealing to us the sinful aspects of our cultural heritages which we should no longer embrace.

As unique reflections of the image of God, every person is inherently equal in the eyes of God. As God's children through Christ, we each uniquely reflect the image of our Father. Just as in earthly parental-child relationships, each of us is "just like" our Father (uniquely reflects His image) in a unique way. We are each His unique child in terms of our individual gifts, talents, and personality, cultural heritage(s), and gender.

As distinct children of God, we also represent distinct parts of the body of Christ. We need each other to learn who God is and to grow in relationship to Him. (1 Corinthians 12:12-31)

At the same time, the distinct image of God in each of us is marred because of sin. (Romans 5: 12-13) Our individual gifts and talents get abused for selfish reasons, our personalities become fractured and distorted, and our cultures and perspectives of gender become tainted because of sin. Through Christ we experience forgiveness and sanctification which draws out the image of God in us more clearly. Our individual gifts and talents become refined and used for God's purposes, our personalities become healed and made whole, the unique and positive aspects of our culture(s) shine brightly, and we gain a godly perspective of the unique ways in which God has made both men and women (1 Corinthians 15: 21-22. Romans 5: 15-19. 2 Corinthians 3: 18).

The closer we draw to Christ, the more and more He sanctifies us and draws out His unique reflection in us, and the more He is glorified. As St. Irenaeus said: "The glory of God is a person fully alive."

I am God's unique child and by His design I uniquely reflect who He is to the world. I'm just like my Daddy in a way that no one in the world ever has been or ever will be. Also, like a mirror, I uniquely reflect who God is to the world. *I uniquely reflect God's image in terms of my personality, gifts, talents, and passions; my gendered background; and, my multi-faceted cultural backgrounds.* I, as a Chinese, Mexican, American, Asian, Chicano, Latino male, together with my distinct individual personality, gifts, talents, and passions, *uniquely reflect the image of God.* Because of Jesus, I am a *unique child of God. And so are you.*

*PraXis*

In Jesus, we find our true identity as a Child of God. Only in Jesus do all of our other sub-identities--based upon race, culture, gender, etc.—find their fulfillment. For example, our racial/cultural background is a beautiful thing, but if we try to base all of our identity upon it, we will always be left unsatisfied. We will also end up excluding others.

Same thing with gender. Gender is a wonderful, God-given attribute, but we're not intended to base all of our identity upon it.

When we surrender our life to Jesus, we become a Child of God, and all of our other sub-identities—including our ethnic, racial, and gender identities--find their fulfillment and ultimate expression.

Have you ever surrendered your life to Jesus and become a Child of God? Jesus is calling…

How do I mirror God
Volunteering
How do I not ---
Language


Brenee Brown
Brian McCleovan
Engage to understand, not
to change . ---

## 14 Manifest Destiny? The Historical Misrepresentation of Christianity

Western imperialism and colonization destroyed the global witness of Christianity. Starting with Columbus in 1492, and well into the 20th century, numerous European nations, together with the United States, went around and ravaged the globe. They used their superior military power to conquer almost every nation in Asia, Africa, the Middle East, and the Americas, and as a consequence, millions of people died. Those that did not die were enslaved, subjugated as forced labor, stripped of their national resources, and treated as second-class citizens in their own countries. To make matters worse, most, if not all of these western nations claimed to be "Christian." Reflecting the perverted religious views of conquest held by many Europeans and Americans in the 19th century, one Rev. Muller stated: "Humanity must not, cannot allow the incompetence, negligence, and laziness of the uncivilized peoples to leave idle indefinitely the wealth which God has confided to them, charging them to make it serve the good of all."[1] In agreement with these racist religious sentiments, one Rev. Barde stated similarly, "[if the goods of this world] remained divided up indefinitely, as they would be without colonization, they would remain without colonization, they would answer neither the purposes of God nor the just demands of the human collectivity."

The destruction caused by colonialism was not limited to some time in the distant past. We *still* feel the terrible consequences of imperialism in the United States and in most nations of the developing world. African Americans, Latinos, and Native Americans continue to experience extraordinary levels of poverty in the United States and to live in communities that are even more segregated than 50 years ago. *Agree* Their families and children continue to suffer from unequal public education systems, lack of affordable housing and healthcare, police brutality, unequal justice in the courts, and pervasive racist stereotypes. Racist socio-economic, legal, and political institutions persist in Latin America, and harmful legacies of colonialism are alive throughout Africa. It is even argued that HIV/AIDS, the most deadly pandemic of our time, may have spread throughout Africa because of European colonization.[2]

As a result of the religious arrogance and social devastation associated with imperialism, millions of people of color throughout the globe have condemned Christianity over the past five centuries as a "white man's, colonizer's religion." "If this is what Christianity is all about," they say, "then why would I ever want to be a Christian?" Or, like Gandhi, they say, "I like your Christ. I do not like your Christians. They are so unlike your Christ." It's hard to blame them for feeling this way.

This negative perspective of Christianity is poignantly articulated in the haunting song, "Sweet Jesus," by the Native American folk group, The Thunderbird Sisters:

> "In the name of your Jesus you came by the boatload,
> proclaiming he showed you the way

Preaching fire and brimstone, hell and damnation,
preaching Jesus commands you obey

Jesus, sweet Jesus, did you really tell them,
to murder my grandma that way

They called her a sinner cause they couldn't win her,
and she drowned in her blood where she lay

In the name of your Jesus, ten thousands of thousands,
of Christians arrived on our shores

They came waving Bibles, crosses and rifles,
building churches on Indian graves

Jesus, sweet Jesus, did you really tell them,
to murder my mother that way

They called her a sinner cause they couldn't win her,
and she drowned in her blood where she lay

Jesus, sweet Jesus, did you really tell them,
to murder my brother that way

They called him a heathen, a savage then shot him and he
drowned in his blood where he lay…."

I am haunted and deeply distressed by the lyrics of this song—
because they are true. At least partially. Jesus did not tell them to kill
her family members, but, contrary to the rosy stories of the pilgrims
and the Thanksgiving holiday myth, English settlers came to this
continent and slaughtered the first nations people that they
encountered. And they called themselves Christians! As I write these
words I am deeply jarred and I think to myself: If this is what
Christians have done, *how can I be a Christian?* If all this stuff is really

166

*Also Japan*

true about justice and diversity being big concerns of God, then why have his self-proclaimed followers *done so many bad things in history?*

Actually, "bad things" is quite an understatement. It's more like *"the most atrocious things you could possibly imagine."*

90% of the indigenous population of the Valley of Mexico *Disease* died within the first hundred years of the Spanish conquest.[3] This bloody conquest was carried out by Spain in the name of "God and Gold." As many as 11 million native Americans also died as part of the various European conquests and colonization efforts in North America.[4] The U.S. carried out its conquest of the western United States as part of a deeply-entrenched religious belief called "Manifest Destiny." According to this twisted ideology, many Anglo Americans felt it was ok to kill Native Americans and seize their lands because they thought it was God's plan for the United States to extend from "sea to shining sea." I can't believe people actually believed this stuff!

In the name of God and Manifest Destiny, the United States also seized more than half of Mexico in 1848 as part of what Abraham Lincoln called an "unjust war." In fact, the young Abraham Lincoln staked his entire early political career as a congressman upon condemnation of the Mexican-American War (or what Mexicans call, the "War of American aggression.") In his words, the war "was unnecessarily and unconstitutionally commenced by the President." He wasn't alone. In his autobiography, General Ulysses S. Grant asserted that the Civil War was God's way of punishing the United States for the injustice of the Mexican-American War. Grant also stated: "I had a horror of the Mexican War…only I had not moral courage enough to resign…I considered my supreme duty was to my flag."

As a specific example of Manifest Destiny as it played itself out on the battlefield, one American volunteer officer stationed in Mexico wrote:

> "I wish I had the power to stop their churches…to bring off this treasure hoard of gold and jewels, and to put the greasy priests, monks, friars and other officials at work on the public highways as a preliminary step to mending their ways…It is perfectly certain that this war is a divine dispensation intended to purify and punish this misguided nation…Most of our officers concur with me that nothing but a divine ruler and commander could have brought us safely through so much peril against awful odds."[5]

Echoing similar wacked-out religious sentiments, another American soldier declared:

> " I cannot help but think, that God has fought upon our side, to chastize them[Mexicans] for their sins."[6]

As a Mexican American, and a Christian, it makes me want to throw up when I read about Manifest Destiny. It also makes me sympathetic to the many Chican@s and Latin@s who reject Christianity after they learn about this insane religious concept which led to the murder and dispossession of thousands of first nations people and Mexicans.

Lest some readers think that I'm just a radical ethnic studies conspiracy theorist, I close my discussion of Manifest Destiny and the

Mexican American War with the following quote from Nicholas Trist. Trist was the U.S. diplomatic representative charged with negotiating the Treaty of Guadalupe-Hidalgo which officially ended the war (incidentally the treaty also led to many more injustices related to land and citizenship, but I'll have to leave that discussion for another time). You could say he was kind of like Hillary Clinton, Secretary of State. Here's what he said:

> "If those Mexicans…had been able to look into my heart at that moment, they would have found that the sincere shame I felt as a North American was stronger than theirs as Mexicans. Although I was unable to say it at the time, it was something that any North American should be ashamed of…"[7]

Since I've broached the topic of the Civil War and God's punishment of the United States for historical injustices, it's worth mentioning that Abraham Lincoln also stated (in his famous 2nd Inaugural Address which is currently plastered across an entire wall of the Lincoln Memorial in Washington, D.C.,) that the Civil War was God's retribution for the injustices of slavery. Specifically, he said that all of the white blood shed as part of the Civil War was God's punishment for all of the black blood shed as part of the evil institution of slavery. Wow! Nobody ever told me about this in my high school U.S. history class.

It gets worse. Many Americans used the Bible (out of context) to justify the terrible institution of slavery for more than three hundred years. They argued that the dark skin of blacks represented the "mark of Cain" and therefore justified the enslavement of African descent individuals. Unconvinced of their folly (and perhaps of the divine retribution spoken of by Lincoln above), many southerners later went on to justify Jim Crow segregation and all of its associated evils using twisted theological reasoning as well. They claimed that, based upon the story of the tower of Babel, it was God's intent to maintain the permanent separation of the races.

Such religiously-justified racism was not limited to the South. Northerners did the same thing. In California, for example, the anti-Chinese movement of the 1870's and 80's was also justified in religious terms. I was horrified when I came across this prayer from a San Francisco pastor, Isaac Kalloch, (who later went on to become mayor). On July 4, 1878 he prayed:

> "We believe, O Lord, that the foundations of our government were laid by Thine own hand; that all the steps and stages of our progress have been under Thy watch and ward...We meet together today to celebrate the anniversary of our national birth, and we pray that we may be enabled to carry out the divine principles which inspired our noble sires and others, and we pray that our rules may be righteous; that our people may be peaceable; that capital may respect the rights of labor, and that labor may honor capital; *that the Chinese must go*...and good men stay. We believe Thou wilt hear our prayer when we pray that we believe to be right."[8]

This quote really says it all. This pastor used Christianity, and his official clerical office, to justify discrimination against Chinese immigrants who came to the U.S. in order to be able to work hard and feed there families, and who were initially recruited to the U.S. to serve as cheap laborers for jobs that nobody else wanted to do. I cringe every time I read this prayer because it is a disgusting misrepresentation of Jesus (I am certain that He cringed as well when He heard this prayer, too). It is also emblematic of the disgusting misrepresentation of Jesus which I find riddled throughout the history of the United States and Latin America (and almost everywhere else on the planet).

For the past five hundred years, people have used Christianity to justify historical oppression based upon race. In this example, the Chinese are the targets, but you could easily replace the word Chinese in this evil prayer with "Mexican," "African-American," "Japanese," "Filipino," "South Asian," or "Middle Eastern." Each of these racial groups (and many others) have experienced historical racism in the United States justified, at least in part, on the basis of so-called Christian theology.

I could go on to cite many more examples of the ways in which Christianity has been used to support racism and sexism, but I will stop here. I think I've made my point:

*Christianity has been used to justify some of the worst forms of race-based discrimination over the past five hundred years.*

*As we'll see in the next chapter, however, there is good news. All that I have just described are misrepresentations of Christianity, and I have found an important historical principle at work throughout Christian history: every time Jesus' name has been misrepresented as a justification for injustice, someone has stepped up to challenge the misrepresentation and to stand for the biblical truths*

*Japan Hindu Islam May all do it*

*But so has Islam, Buddhism, Hinduism, etc.*

171

*which we have discussed throughout this book—Justice and diversity are at the center of God's heart.*

*PraXis*

Have you or someone you know fallen away from faith because of historical misrepresentations of Christianity? Read on for the good news…

# 15 God Never Leaves Himself Without A Witness: MLK, Cesar Chavez, and other Social Justice Pioneers

God is a God of justice and diversity. As discussed at great length in chapter 1, more than 2,000 Bible verses declare emphatically that God loves the poor and is angered by injustice. As we talked about in chapters 2-5, God loves immigrants and offers stern warnings against their exploitation. Finally, as we've discussed in chapters 9-13, God is the author of human diversity, and every human being uniquely reflects His image in terms of their individual gifts, talents, personality, gender, and cultural heritage.

I am comforted by these biblical truths every time I find myself angered by historical and contemporary misrepresentations of Jesus like the ones discussed in the previous chapter. As a historian, I'm also encouraged by an important principle I've seen at work in global history: *Every time Christianity has been misrepresented to the world as a racist, classist, and sexist religion, sincere followers of Jesus have forcefully challenged the misrepresentation and declared emphatically that God is a God of justice and compassion.* Just as important, they have acted upon these convictions and changed the world. This inspires me and makes me hopeful. If God is really a God of justice, should we really be surprised?

The goal of this chapter, and the next, is to highlight some of my Christian heroes who have championed racial and socioeconomic justice over the past 2,000 years.

## Las Casas

My favorite historical example of a Christian social justice revolutionary is Bartolomé de las Casas. Las Casas lived during the Spanish Conquest of Mexico and Latin America. Like all of us, he was not a perfect man, but, more than anyone I can think of, he was God's witness to the fact that the Spanish Conquest was *wrong and a travesty of justice.*[1] Prior to his radical conversion, Las Casas participated in the Spanish conquest of what is today Cuba, and for his efforts was rewarded richly by the Crown. One day in 1514, Las Casas read the following words from the Apocryphal text of Ecclesiasticus 34:21-22, and his life was never again the same:

> "The bread of the needy is their life, he that defraudeth him thereof is a man of blood. He that taketh away his neighbour's living slayeth him, and he that defraudeth the labourer of his hire is a bloodshedder."

These words pierced his soul and caused him to reflect upon the profound injustices that he and other Spaniards had committed against the native populations of the Americas. He also hearkened back to a sermon he had heard three years earlier by Dominican Friar Antonio Montesinos which preached on the Sunday before Christmas on the island of Hispaniola:

> "With what right, and with what justice do you keep these poor Indians in such cruel and horrible servitude? By what authority have you made such detestable wars against these people who lived peacefully and gently on their own

lands? Are these not men? Do they not have rational souls? Are you not obliged to love them as yourselves?"[2]

Las Casas spent many days reflecting upon the plight of the natives until he had a deep spiritual conversion and "determined within himself of the same truth, that everything which had been done to the Indians in the Indies was unjust and tyrannical." He gave up his money and his wealth and devoted the rest of his life to the condemnation of the Spanish Conquest and advocacy on behalf of the native populations. He eventually joined the Dominican Order himself, became Bishop of Chiapas, and received the official title "Defender of the Indians." He wrote a famous book called, *A Short Account of the Destruction of the Indies*, which described in detail the horrors and unbiblical evils associated with the Spanish colonization of the Caribbean. The purpose of the book was to document the historical atrocities which had taken place in the New World and to warn that God would destroy the Spanish nation if it did not repent of its oppressive imperialism. In a sense, *A Short of Account of the Destruction of the Indies* can be considered one of the first ethnic studies texts because it sought to preserve the history of an oppressed minority group and to use this history to advocate for social change.[3]

Las Casas' writings and advocacy efforts prompted what was called the "Great Debate" in Spain. From 1550-51, Las Casas debated theologian Juan Gines de Sepúlveda over the biblical justifications for the conquest. Las Casas argued that the Conquest was unjust and biblical, and Sepúlveda asserted the opposite position. Beyond this specific debate in the royal courts, Las Casas also inspired a broader public debate in Spain over the validity of the Conquest.

In my mind, Las Casas was also the first Latino labor organizer. In addition to arguing against the injustice of the Spanish Conquest in general, he also successfully advocated for the "New Laws" which abolished Indian slavery and dismantled an entire forced labor system known as the encomienda. He was so radical that he even withheld the sacraments from Spaniards who held Indians and did not properly compensate them for their labor. He was also reprimanded for denying last rights to an a Spanish landowner or "encomendero."

Three hundred years before the abolition of slavery in the U.S., Las Casas even denounced African slavery.

I love Las Casas because he clearly illustrates the historical principle at the heart of this whole chapter: *Jesus never leaves himself without a witness. Every time Jesus' name has been misrepresented in history, God has raised up a Las Casas to clear the record and show the world that justice is at the center of Jesus' heart.*

Here are some other examples of people from history who have stood for God's justice in the face of opposition from others who called themselves Christian:

*The Early Church (Pentecost-4th Century A.D.)*
The earliest followers of Jesus were *defined* by their love and concern for the poor. Love and justice were not a peripheral part of their agenda. On the contrary, love for the dispossessed of society was what

made them stand out from the rest. Their rallying cry was not "you're poor because you're lazy," or, "equal opportunity, but not equal results" as many Christians in America might say today. Instead it was, "Jesus commands us to love the poor and our neighbors as ourselves, and so we will do."

In fact, as Henry Chadwick states, love for the poor was likely the single most important factor which accounted for the rapid spread of Christianity in its early years:

> "The practical application of charity was probably the most potent single cause of Christian success [in the early church]. The pagan comment 'See how these Christians love one another' (reported by Tertullian) was not irony. Christian charity expressed itself in care for the poor, for widows and orphans, in visits to brethren in prison or condemned to the living death of labour in the mines, and in social action in time of calamity like famine, earthquake, pestilence, or war."[4]

Moreover, according to Chadwick, the early church recognized that the primary role of church finances was to provide for the special needs of the poor! As a pioneering force for social justice, moreover, the early Christians even protested the institution of slavery in the fourth century![5]

Ebherhard Arnold fills in this amazing picture of the early Christians by describing how they used to go street-by-street in search of the poorest and most destitute:

"[E]ven in the smallest Church community the overseer had to be a friend of the poor, and there had to be at least one widow responsible to see to it, day and night, that no sick or needy person was neglected. To inquire into and locate poverty and to impress on the rich the need to do their utmost was the deacons' service, which was combined with the service at table. Nor was it an excuse for any other Christian that he had not learned to do this service or was unable to perform this task. *Everybody was expected to seek out, street by street, the poorest dwellings of strangers, with the result that the Christians spent more money in the streets than the followers of other religions spent in their temples. Working for the destitute was, then, what distinguished the first Christians...*What struck and astounded the outside observer most was the extent to which poverty was overcome in the vicinity of the communities."[6]

Did you catch that, "everybody was expected to seek out, street by street, the poorest dwellings of strangers" in order to minister to the poor! What an incredible and inspiring witness! Forgive us Lord for how far we have strayed from the early church's example.

As a way of closing my brief discussion of the early church, I hope that you might be inspired by the following quotations taken from historical primary source documents. In the words of the early church itself, and its observers, these passages remind us of how important love for the poor was to those who were most closely connected to Jesus in both time and space.

"Happiness does not consist in ruling over one's neighbors or in longing to have more than one's weaker fellowmen. Nor does it consist in being rich and in oppressing those lowlier than oneself. No one can imitate God by doing such things. They are alien to His sublimity. *On the contrary, anyone who takes his neighbor's burden upon himself, who tries to help the weaker one in points where he has an advantage, who gives what he has received from God to those who need it, takes God's place, as it were, in the eyes of those who receive it."* [7]

*...If anyone among them is poor or comes in want while they themselves have nothing to spare, they fast two or three days for him. In this way they can supply any poor man with the food he needs...Their life is one of consecration and justice."* [8]

*"We who formerly treasured money and possessions more than anything else now hand over everything we have to a treasury for all and share it with everyone who needs it.* We who formerly hated and murdered one another and did not even share our hearth with those of a different tribe because of their customs, now, after Christ's appearance, live together and share the same table."[9]

"My child, flee from every evil thing, and from every likeness of it... *Be neither money-loving, nor vainglorious, for out of all these thefts are engendered."*[10]

*"And the way of death is this:* First of all it is evil and accursed: murders, adultery, lust, fornication, thefts, idolatries, magic arts, witchcrafts, rape, false witness, hypocrisy, double-heartedness, deceit, haughtiness, depravity, self-will, *greediness,* filthy talking, jealousy, over-confidence, loftiness, boastfulness; persecutors of the good, hating truth, loving a lie, not knowing a reward for righteousness, not cleaving to good nor to righteous judgment, watching not for that which is good, but for that which is evil; from whom meekness and endurance are far, loving vanities, pursuing revenge, *not pitying a poor man, not laboring for the afflicted, not knowing Him Who made them,* murderers of children, destroyers of the handiwork of God, *turning away from him who is in want,* afflicting him who is distressed, *advocates of the rich, lawless judges of the poor, utter sinners. Be delivered, children, from all these."*[11]

*Roger Williams:* pastor and founder of present-day Rhode Island, Williams protested against the unjust colonization of Native American lands by English settlers. He criticized English colonization efforts as unjust and illegal, and maintained that the lands occupied by Puritan settlers rightly belonged to the Native Americans. As founder of the colony of Providence, Williams settled with a group of friends on lands he purchased from Native Americans. He also founded the Baptist Church in America.[12]

*Abolitionist Movement:* Christians were at the forefront of the global abolition movement. In 1776, the Quakers expelled all slaveholders from their congregations. Moravian Christians from what is now the Czech Republic sold themselves into slavery in order to minister to African slaves.

William Wilberforce spearheaded the anti-slavery movement in England which led to the abolition of slavery in Britain, and eventually, in most of the western world.[13] During this same time, Methodists and Quakers were influential in the promotion of prison reform, child labor laws, and labor unions.[14]

*Lucretia Mott:* was a Christian and leader of the women's suffrage movement in the United States. She organized the Seneca Falls Convention in 1848 which marked the origins of the women's suffrage movement in the U.S.[15]

*César E. Chávez:* along with Dolores Huerta, Chávez was one of the central leaders of the Chicano farm workers movement. Unknown to most, he was a devout follower of Jesus who also admired the writings of the Apostle Paul. At Friday night meetings at the United Farm Workers headquarters in Delano, he would pray and often share inspiring insights from the Bible. Prior to important rallies, Chávez would also celebrate mass. He learned the biblical basis for community organizing from a Catholic priest, Father Donald McDonnell, who he shadowed for a number of years. His famous hunger strike of 1968, was a spiritual fast aimed at invoking God's intervention into the grid-locked farmworker negotiations. It worked.

Speaking of his faith in Christ, César Chávez once said: "Today I don't think I could base my will to struggle on cold economics or on some political doctrine. I don't think there would be enough to sustain me. For me the base must be faith." [16] "The only justice is Christ—God's justice. We're the victims of a lot of shenanigans by the courts but ultimately, down the line, real justice comes. It does not come from the courts, but it comes from a set of circumstances and I think God's hand is in it. God tends to write very straight with crooked lines."[17]


*Rev. Martin Luther King, Jr.*: Rev. King needs little introduction, but he was a Baptist minister and follower of Jesus. For his leadership of the movement which led to the end of de jure racial segregation in America, Rev. King received the Nobel Peace prize in 1964. In a famous sermon at Ebenezer Baptist Church in Atlanta in 1968, Dr. King spoke about Jesus' unmatched transformative role in human history:

"I know a man — and I just want to talk about him a minute, and maybe you will discover who I'm talking about as I go down the way because he was a great one. And he just went about serving. He was born in an obscure village, the child of a poor peasant woman. And then he grew up in still another obscure village, where he worked as a carpenter until he was thirty years old. Then for three years, he just got on his feet, and he was an itinerant preacher. And he went about doing some things. He didn't have much. He never wrote a book. He never held an office. He never had a family. He never owned a house. He never went to college...He did none of the usual things that the world would associate with greatness. He had no credentials but himself.

> He was only thirty-three when the tide of public opinion turned against him. They called him a rabble-rouser. They called him a troublemaker. They said he was an agitator. He practiced civil disobedience; he broke injunctions. And so he was turned over to his enemies and went through the mockery of a trial...Nineteen centuries have come and gone and today he stands as the most influential figure that ever entered human history. All of the armies that ever marched, all the navies that ever sailed, all the parliaments that ever sat, and all the kings that ever reigned put together have not affected the life of man on this earth (Amen) as much as that one solitary life."[18]

In his famous, "A Letter from Birmingham Jail," Dr. King also warned the Christian church in America about God's coming judgment if it did not rise up and stand for racial justice[19]:

"So often the contemporary church is a weak, ineffectual voice with an uncertain sound. So often it is an archdefender of the status quo. Far from being disturbed by the presence of the church, the power structure of the average community is consoled by the church's silent and often even vocal sanction of things as they are.

> But the judgment of God is upon the church as never before. If today's church does not recapture the sacrificial spirit of the early church, it will lose its authenticity, forfeit the loyalty of millions, and be dismissed as an irrelevant social club with no meaning for the twentieth century."

Very importantly for purposes of our discussion, King also noted that he had encountered many college students who left the organized church because of the church's failure to support the civil rights movements:

> "Every day I meet young people whose disappointment with the church has turned into outright disgust."

As part of his persuasive rhetoric, Dr. King also invoked the example of the early church, which was noted for its commitment to social justice issues and love for the poor and dispossessed:

> "There was a time when the church was very powerful in the time when the early Christians rejoiced at being deemed worthy to suffer for what they believed. In those days the church was not merely a thermometer that recorded the ideas and principles of popular opinion; it was a thermostat that transformed the mores of society.

Whenever the early Christians entered a town, the people in power became disturbed and immediately sought to convict the Christians for being "disturbers of the peace" and "outside agitators." But the Christians pressed on, in the conviction that they were "a colony of heaven," called to obey God rather than man. Small in number, they were big in commitment. They were too God intoxicated to be "astronomically intimidated." By their effort and example they brought an end to such ancient evils as infanticide and gladiatorial contests."

Perhaps more than any other historical figure of the 20th century, Rev. Dr. Martin Luther King, Jr. proves that faith and justice go hand in hand; indeed, that for followers of Jesus, they must.

*Oscar Romero:* was a Catholic Bishop who challenged the political and economic corruption of El Salvador in the 1980's. He was martyred for his biblical pursuit of justice. Like King, he preached that it is the responsibility of every Christian to love and advocate on behalf of the poor:

"We must not seek the child Jesus
in the pretty figures of our Christmas cribs.

We must seek him among the undernourished children
who have gone to bed at night with nothing to eat,
among the poor newsboys
who will sleep covered with newspapers in doorways.

God's reign is already present on our earth in mystery.
When the Lord comes, it will be brought to perfection.
That is the hope that inspires Christians.

We know that every effort to better society,

especially when injustice and sin are so ingrained,
is an effort that God blesses, that God wants,
that God demands of us."[20]

*Dietrich Bonhoeffer and the "Confessing Church"*: was established by German Christians to oppose the Nazi regime of Adolph Hitler. Christians created clandestine networks in Germany, France, and various countries in Eastern Europe to help Jews escape from the Nazis. A pastor and leader of the "Confessing Church," Dietrich Bonhoeffer returned to Germany from the U.S. in the 1930's to opposed the Nazi regime. He ran an underground Christian seminary which was shut down by the Gestapo. He was hanged by the Nazis for his opposition to Adolph Hitler.[21] Bonhoeffer is one of President Barack Obama's favorite authors.

*Mother Teresa:* Mother Teresa also needs little introduction. Born in Skopje, Macedonia of Albanian parents, Mother Teresa dedicated her life to serving and loving the poorest of the slums of Calcutta, India. She founded the Missionaries of Charity order in 1950, and today, this Christian order has branches in Asia, Africa, Latin America, North America, Europe, Australia, and Eastern Europe. She was quoted as saying that her work was not social work, but religious work. Mother Teresa was honored with the Nobel Peace Prize in 1979.[22]

Here are some of her famous quotes which capture succinctly and profoundly Jesus' heart for justice and love for the poor:

"Jesus appears in the distressing disguise of the poor."

"The dying, the cripple, the mental,
the unwanted, the unloved
they are Jesus in disguise."

"I try to give to the poor people for love what the rich could get for money. No, I wouldn't touch a leper for a thousand pounds; yet I willingly cure him for the love of God."

"If you can't feed a hundred people, then feed just one."

I could go on and on, but I think you are getting my point (and I hope getting inspired) by now:

*The historical abuses discussed in the previous chapter are misrepresentations of Christianity. Justice is at the center of God's heart. Every time He has been misrepresented in history, sincere followers of Jesus have arisen to challenge the status quo and to stand for biblical justice and equality.*

In the next chapter we'll look at modern day Christian revolutionaries who have continued in this powerful historical tradition...

*PraXis*

1.      Who was your favorite Christian historical figure discussed in this chapter? Why are they your favorite?

2.      Many people fall away from faith because they read about historical misrepresentations of Christianity. After reading this chapter, what would you tell them?

3.    MLK's "Letter from a Birmingham Jail," is a classic writing of the civil rights movement. I highly encourage you to read it in its entirety and reflect upon its significance for today:

www.africa.upenn.edu/Articles_Gen/Letter_Birmingham.htm

4.    Bishop Oscar Romero's sermons are a hidden treasure for Christian activists. Take some time to check them out:

www.plough.com/en/ebooks/uv/violence-of-love

# 16    Modern-Day Revolutionaries

As a crucial part of my journey in reconciling faith with justice, *I have had the privilege of getting to know many individuals and organizations—modern day revolutionaries--who live out the biblical call to justice in a radical way.* They shatter all the negative stereotypes of Christianity that we've discussed in previous chapters by the way they live their lives for Jesus. They are "hidden heroes" of the faith because few people know about them outside of their specific spheres of ministry influence. True to the famous poem by Gil Scott-Heron, this Revolution "has not been televised."

The main goal of this chapter is to introduce you to some of these heroes of the faith (There are undoubtedly many more out there, and I apologize in advance to my brothers and sisters who have been left out of my brief discussion here. With your help, one of my hopes is to greatly expand this list in the future).

Another goal is to bring the topic of justice and God's love for the poor out of the abstract and into the practical. I hope that one, or many, of these organizations might grab your attention, and that you can get plugged in with them and start serving! I've grouped these "heroes of the faith" below by subject matter and organization. I've also included a simplified list of these people and organizations, together with reading suggestions, in Appendix II. *Buena suerte.*

*Christian Community Development and the CCDA*

Are you interested in serving the poor on a local level? Are you interested in community development? Would you enjoy mentoring inner city youth and helping bring jobs and affordable housing to urban communities? Could you see yourself practicing law or medicine in a community of need? Are you interested in gang intervention work? If you said yes to any of these questions, then Christian Community Development is for you!

The Christian Community Development Association (CCDA) is an amazing organization representing thousands of inner city Christian ministries in the United States and abroad. CCDA ministries are involved in every type of community development work that you can imagine—education, housing, alleviating homelessness, public health, law, advocacy for undocumented immigrants, microfinance, and on and on and on. The CCDA will blow your mind. The CCDA was founded by amazing African-American community development and civil rights pioneer John Perkins. It's now led by a Chicano and Chicagoan--Noel Castellanos. http://www.ccda.org/

Here is a description of the CCDA taken from their website:

The Christian Community Development Association (CCDA) is a network of Christians committed to seeing people and communities "wholistically" restored. We believe that God wants to restore us not only to right relationship with Himself but also with our own true selves, our families and our communities. Not just spiritually, but emotionally, physically, economically, and socially. Not by offering mercy alone, but by undergirding mercy with justice.

To this end, we follow Jesus's example of reconciliation. We go where the brokenness is. We live among the people in some of America's neediest neighborhoods. We become one with our neighbors until there is no longer an "us" and "them" but only a "we." And, in the words of the Prophet Jeremiah, "we work and pray for the well-being of our city [or neighborhood]," trusting that if the entire community does well and prospers, then we will prosper also.

Stated succinctly, *the vision* of the CCDA is:

"Wholistically" restored communities with Christians fully engaged in the process of transformation.

Their *mission* is:

"To inspire, train, and connect Christians who seek to bear witness to the Kingdom of God by reclaiming and restoring under-resourced communities."

Christian community development is an entire culture and community of Jesus followers who live in inner cities throughout the world and love the poor. They become part of the communities in which they live and resist the "ride in on a white horse" mentality of many organizations. Instead, they choose to learn from their neighbors, come along side the good work that God is already doing in urban communities, and foster "indigenous leadership" from the community itself.

An entire CCDA literature has developed over the years, and CCDA pioneers like John Perkins, Bob Lupton, and Ray Bakke have authored numerous books about inner city ministry and the philosophy behind Christian community development. There are literally hundreds of wonderful books about Christian Community Development to read and learn from. We've assembled a list of good CCDA reads for you in Appendix II.

My favorite part of the CCDA is their annual conference. Every year the CCDA descends upon a major U.S. city and has a huge gathering involving thousands of participants from throughout the country (and world) and top-notch speakers. In addition to the amazing plenary sessions, they have dozens of smaller break-out sessions where you can learn about all the cutting-edge ministry that is going on related to law, housing, education, medicine, immigration…you name it. I encourage every reader of this book to go to at least one CCDA conference. It will blow you away!

Did I make you interested? Check out the CCDA! http://www.ccda.org/

*Urban Youth Workers: The S.A.Y. Yes! Centers for Youth Development and the UYWI*

Urban youth ministry is a central component of Christian community development. All throughout the country, thousands of followers of Christ live in inner city communities and mentor youth as part of church youth groups and after-school programs. From first-hand experience, I know that the lives of thousands of kids are transformed every year because of the dedication and service of thousands of urban youth workers. My wife was one of them. For more than 15 years she lived and served in South L.A. as part of the "S.A.Y. Yes! Centers for Youth Development (now, Cru YouthDev). (http://www.sayyescenters.org/). I'm proud to say that she was also one of the founding team members for this organization which now has hundreds of affiliates throughout the U.S. and even in India and Latin America (She'll never tell you this but its my God-given responsibility as her husband to do so!).

S.A.Y. Yes! is a program of an urban ministry called Here's Life Inner City (HLIC, now known as the Inner City Ministry of Cru) which has branches throughout the country. As part of S.A.Y. Yes!, HLIC partners with inner city churches to start after school programs. Here's a description of S.A.Y. Yes taken from their website:

In many inner-city neighborhoods, Christians are feeling a need to open the doors of their churches during the after school hours, and to minister to children and teens during this time of day when many are unsupervised and vulnerable to getting into trouble. The S.A.Y. Yes! program of HLIC is designed to minister to the wholistic needs of young people: physical, spiritual, emotional, social and intellectual. Here's Life Inner City offers specialized training, curriculum, and other forms of assistance.

My favorite S.A.Y. Yes! Centers are the ones sponsored by the Nehemiah House in the Pico Union District of Los Angeles (www.evfreela.org/#/nehemiah-house/the-nh-internship), Central City Church in the heart of L.A.'s Skid Row (www.lacentralcity.org/), Westside Vineyard in Los Angeles ([www.vcfwestside.org/657900.ihtml](www.vcfwestside.org/657900.ihtml)), and the Agape Center in Chicago ([www.hlicchicago.org/#](www.hlicchicago.org/#)).

The S.A.Y. Yes! Centers for Youth Development, or Cru YouthDev, are only one of many types of similar Christian urban youth programs throughout the country. Examples of others include, the Harambee Center and School in Pasadena ([www.harambeeministries.org/](www.harambeeministries.org/)),"La Villita" in Chicago ([www.lavillitacommunitychurch.com/](www.lavillitacommunitychurch.com/)), and Kidworks in Santa Ana ([kidworksonline.org/](kidworksonline.org/)).

Urban youth workers are connected not only by the CCDA, but also by a fantastic organization called the Urban Youth Workers Institute. The UYWI was founded by Latino community development pioneer Larry Acosta, and it's a sister organization to the CCDA. It is kind of like CCDA's "cool younger brother." The UYWI provides workshops, trainings, and resources for urban youth workers throughout the United States. Here is their mission, vision, and statement of values:

> MISSION: For urban youth to have the leaders and role models they need to live transformed live by the Gospel of Jesus Christ
>
> VISION: To train urban leaders with a priority in 250 of America's at-risk zip codes by 2015.
>
> VALUES: Christ-centered, Holistic, Relational, Multi-ethnic, Collaborative, Relevant

As their name implies, the UYWI is on the frontlines of urban youth work in American.  Check them out! http://uywi.org/

*Soccer for Social Change and Compton United*

One innovative approach to youth development involves the use of soccer.   A close friend of mine, Mike Herman, has been on the forefront of soccer youth development through his organizations, Compton United and Soccer for Social Change.  These orgs use the sport of soccer to holistically mentor youth—spiritually, educationally, physically, and emotionally--and they have many amazing success stories!  For more info, see:

www.comptonunited.org/

www.soccerforsocialchange.com/

*Hip Hop Youth Development: CryOut!*

Another exciting niche among urban youth workers involves the use of Hip Hop as a tool for mentorship.  There are a number of great organizations which do this, but I'd like to spotlight one called "CryOut!"  CryOut! was begun by one of our former CSC students, Celestine Ezinkwo, together with his wife Tara.  "CryOut! exists to develop youth leaders who live freely and pursue justice for those who are oppressed in their communities, their cities and the world. We use creative platforms such as music, dance, arts and workshops focused on life and creative skills to empower the youth." For more info, see: www.celestinerap.com/cryout.

For a great read on the relationship between Christianity and hip hop, check out:

*The Soul of Hip Hop: Rims, Timbs & Cultural Theology*. Daniel White Hodge. 2010.

*Heaven Has a Ghetto: The Missiological Gospel & Theology of Tupac Amaru Shakur*. Daniel White Hodge. 2009.

*Jesus & the Hip-Hop Prophets: Spiritual Insights from Lauryn Hill and 2Pac* by John Teter and Alex Gee. 2003.

For some good hip hop, give a listen to one of some our former CSC students:

Jon Serrins: www.youtube.com/watch?v=IMHOzvtlLeo

Celestine: www.youtube.com/user/celestinerap

Izakela: www.youtube.com/watch?v=FWmjXDzfEhc

*Here's Life Inner City (HLIC), Servant Partners, Mission Waco, and Metro Community Development Corporation, Lighthouse Community Outreach*

HLIC (now known as Inner City Ministry of Cru) and Servant Partners are two fantastic organizations which promote Christian community development in the United States and throughout the globe. HLIC is a nation-wide Christian community development organization which partners with urban churches to bring holistic change to inner city communities. They have branches in NYC, Los Angeles, Seattle, Denver, Minneapolis, Orlando, Chicago, Detroit, Milwaukee, and the Twin Cities. My wife lived in South L.A. and worked with HLIC for

197

15 years. HLIC is the urban ministry of Cru (formerly known as Campus Crusade for Christ). http://www.hlic.org/

Servant Partners is another wonderful Christian organization which focuses upon community development and church planting. I love their name. I think their name captures what true Christian urban ministry is all about. As followers of Jesus, we don't "parachute" into communities of need as outside saviors. No, we humbly "partner" with the indigenous leaders of urban communities and are there to "serve." Servant Partners has branches in Los Angeles and San Antonio, but also in a variety of global locations such as Bangkok, Thailand, Johannesburg, South Africa, Mexico City, Mexico, North Africa, and the Middle East. Servant Partners shares close ties to InterVarsity Christian Fellowship. www.servantpartners.org/

Mission Waco is a fabulous organization in Waco, Texas led by Jimmy and Janet Dorrell. Mission Waco does all manner of community development work in Texas and abroad. They are known especially for creating "the Poverty Simulation," where participants learn about God's love for the poor by simulating being homeless for several days. I've done the poverty simulation a couple of times in Los Angeles and it's life-changing! www.missionwaco.org/homeindex.html

Metro Community Development Corp. is an amazing Christian community development organization dedicated to loving and serving the City of Compton. It's led by our close friends Bob and Susan Combs, and Mike and Tonya Herman. Here's their mission:

"We believe God is in the midst of rebirthing Compton into a new city. Our mission is to be a part of His work, employing whole-life discipleship, asset-based community development, and "business as mission" (to empower individuals, build families, and strengthen neighborhoods).

A unique aspect of the Metro CDC is its use of business as a strategic tool to help transform the city. As examples of their innovative approach to ministry, Metro CDC sells used cars, mentors youth through the construction trade (they are remodeling my kitchen as we speak!), and is currently creating the only urban community garden in South L.A. For more info, see: http://www.metrocdc.org/

I also wanted to give a shout-out to Pastor Greg Bynum and the Lighthouse Community Outreach in Watts. Pastor Greg and staff have been doing amazing community development for 15 years—with much effect but not much recognition. He left a comfortable job as an engineer to become part of Watts and to love the community. That's what it's all about. http://lighthousewatts.com/

*Sojourners*

Sojourners was founded by Rev. Jim Wallis many years ago to pursue God's heart for justice by doing all of the things we've talked about in this book. The organization is named after African-American abolitionist and women's rights activist, Sojourner Truth. Jim Wallis has written many wonderful books about God and the pursuit of justice (cited in the Appendix). Sojourners is involved with national and international level advocacy around the many issues of justice, including human trafficking, undocumented immigrant rights, fair trade, etc.    Sojourners also publishes a monthly magazine and sponsors an influential blog called "God's Politics." http://sojo.net/

*The Justice Conference*

The Justice Conference is another great organization which puts on a fantastic conference centered upon the theme of faith and justice. Unlike the CCDA which is focused upon community development, the Justice Conference explores a broader variety of themes related to race, human trafficking, the arts, etc.    The Justice Conference was founded by World Relief and Kilns College, and its annual conference draws a wide range of  support from many Christian organizations. http://thejusticeconference.com

*InterVarsity Christian Fellowship:  Social Justice League and Fresno Institute for Urban Leadership*

InterVarsity Christian Fellowship is at the forefront of student ministries dealing with issues of race and justice.  I have a warm spot in my heart for IV because my grandfather started IV in China in the 1930's and I used to be the faculty advisor for IV at UCLA.    From inner city summer projects like the Los Angeles Urban Project (or "LAUP"), to racial-reconciliation dialogues, to spring break border consciousness trips, IV is leading the way.    IV has even started a "Social Justice League" (http://ivjusticeleague.wordpress.com/) and a special community development program in central California called the "Fresno Institute for Urban Leadership"(http://www.fiful.org/).

To read more about the variety of programs and ministries that IV has to offer, see: http://www.intervarsity.org/.

*Culturally Diverse Campus Ministries*
InterVarsity and Cru also sponsor ethnically diverse student ministries. They celebrate the ethnic cultures of university students while at the same time strive to promote racial reconciliation and solidarity among all students. Here are some orgs which I've had the privilege of learning about and working with over the years:

> *Latino Campus Orgs:*
>> Destino: http://destinomovement.com/
>> LaFe:    http://mem.intervarsity.org/lafe

> *African American Campus Orgs*
>> Impact:
>>> www.cru.org/ministries-and-locations/ministries/the-impact-movement/index.htm
>> Black Campus Ministries:
>>> http://mem.intervarsity.org/bcm

> *Asian American Campus Orgs*
>> EPIC:   http://www.epicmovement.com/
>> Asian American Ministries:
>>> http://mem.intervarsity.org/aam

*Promoting A Culturally Diverse Church*

Increasingly, the Christian church in America is realizing that diversity is one of its biggest strengths and that it is vital to promote cultural unity within its ranks. I know of two special organizations which are devoted to these specific goals:

*Renew Partnerships:* http://renewpartnerships.org/about/

*Accord1:* www.accord1.org/

*Blogs on Race, Justice, and Christianity*

Christina Cleveland: Social Psychology+Faith+Reconciliation
www.christenacleveland.com/

Here's a great Top 25 List of People of Color put together by Christena, too:

www.christenacleveland.com/2013/08/people-of-color-blog-too/

Julie J. Park: Shei Shi Ni De Baba
http://juliepark.wordpress.com/

Yo Soy Kristy: http://yosoykristy.com/

Minister Different: http://ministerdifferent.com/

Scott Crocker: http://crockerchronicle.blogspot.com/

Bruce Reyes-Chow (fellow Asian-Latino!):
http://reyes-chow.com/

Vivian Mabuni (cancer survivor): http://vivianmabuni.com/

Drew G.I. Hart: Taking Jesus Seriously…A Black Anabaptist Perspective http://drewgihart.com/

Urban Faith: http://www.urbanfaith.com/

Enuma Okoro: www.patheos.com/blogs/enumaokoro/

Natasha Robinson: http://asistasjourney.com/

Efrem Smith (hip-hop and culture):

www.efremsmith.com/category/blog/category/blog/

Eugene Cho: http://eugenecho.com/

Robyn Afrik: http://afrikadvantage.com/category/blog/

By Their Strange Fruit:

http://bytheirstrangefruit.blogspot.com/

Brian Foulks: http://syncopatedhustle.com/

Red Letter Christians: www.redletterchristians.org/

Jesus for Revolutionaries (my blog!):

www.jesusforrevolutionaries.org/


*Gender*

Christians for Biblical Equality (CBE): CBE is the best organization I know of which critically, and biblically, examines the relationship between gender and Christianity. Their website is a gateway to many wonderful resources: http://www.cbeinternational.org/


*The Salvation Army*

The Salvation Army needs no introduction, least of all from me. But, it's worth restating that they are the "OG" Christian social justice and community development organization. In addition to ringing little red bells at Christmas time, they do incredible community development work throughout the United States and the world. They are also one of the most well-respected disaster relief organizations, faith-based or secular, on the planet. I'd be tempted to join if I didn't have to wear one of those little suits.

www.salvationarmyusa.org/usn/www_usn_2.nsf/vw-local/Home

### "Faith-Rooted" Community Organizing

Are you a budding community organizer with dreams of becoming the next Dolores Huerta, César Chávez, or Rev. Dr. Martin Luther King, Jr.? "Faith-rooted community organizing" is a new and ground-breaking organizing model developed by Rev. Alexia Salvatierra.

Rev. Salvatierra is a Chicana community organizer who has devoted her life to advocating on behalf of immigrants and the poor in the United States and abroad. She was a lead organizer of both the "Sanctuary movement" in the 1980's and the more recent "New Sanctuary movement."[1]

Drawing from her many years of community organizing experience in the United States, Latin America, and the Philippines, Rev. Salvatierra has pioneered an alternative model of organizing called, "Faith-Rooted Community Organizing." This model places faith at the center, and is an alternative to the popular "Alinsky" model. Rev. Salvatierra has conducted trainings on faith-rooted community organizing for the CCDA, InterVarsity Christian Fellowship, and Biola University. For more information, visit: http://clueca.org/Faith-Rooted_Organizing.html

Rev. Salvatierra used to be executive director of a wonderful faith-based organization called "C.L.U.E. (Clergy and Laity United For Economic Justice.). C.L.U.E. was founded by Rev. James Lawson who was known as Rev. Martin Luther King, Jr.'s "theologian of non-violence." In addition to its important organizing efforts surrounding the issue of undocumented immigration, C.L.U.E. is primarily a faith-based labor organizing 501(c)(3). It is also an "ecumenical" religious organization.

There's C.L.U.E. L.A.: http://cluela.org/

And, C.L.U.E. Orange County:

www.clueoc.org/CLUE_Orange_County/Home.html

C.L.U.E. Orange County has a specifically evangelical flair to it (in a good way!)

Some other faith-based community organizing groups:

PICO California- People Improving Communities through Organizing

PICO California is the largest grassroots congregation-based community-organizing network in California. http://www.picocalifornia.org/

Gameliel http://www.gamaliel.org/

"a grassroots network of non-partisan, faith-based organizations in 17 U.S. states, South Africa and the United Kingdom, that organizes to empower ordinary people to effectively participate in the political, environmental, social and economic decisions affecting their lives."

DART – Direct Action and Research Training Center

http://www.thedartcenter.org/

(Training for congregation-based community organizing)


IAF (Industrial Areas Foundation)

http://www.industrialareasfoundation.org/

(partners with religious congregations and civic organizations at the local level to build broad-based organizing projects)


*Homeless Ministry*

3.5 million people are homeless in America. 39% of them are children. 50% of homeless women and children are on the streets because they are fleeing from domestic abuse. No safe place to lay their head. Little food. Poor education. No healthcare. No one, and especially no child should have to live like this.[2]

Thankfully, many followers of Jesus have stepped up to create ministries that care for homeless people. Here is just a few; there are many more:


Union Rescue Mission   www.urm.org

Central City Community Outreach   www.lacentralcity.org

Central City is especially amazing because it also has a church which is run for, and by, the homeless or formerly homeless. They even have a karaoke night!

Door of Hope   www.doorofhope.us

Especially for families; in Pasadena, California.

Fred Jordan Missions   www.fjm.org

Malachi Clothing

In an interesting spin on traditional homeless ministry, *Malachi Clothing* takes the proceeds of its clothing sales and creates care packages of basic necessities for the homeless community. After a customer has made a purchase, they receive a bracelet and specific prayer request which was given by the individual who received the care package. http://malachiclothing.com/pages/about-us-v1/

*Global Justice and Community Development--World Vision and World Relief*
If I could work for any organization in the world I would work for World Vision (hint, hint if there's anyone from World Vision reading this book!). I would feel very rewarded in life if I were to give all my money to World Vision and engage in no other form of ministry. World Vision provides food, clothing, clean water, and education for thousands of children throughout the world. For less than a dollar a day, as their commercials say, you can sponsor a child. We are privileged to sponsor children from Mexico, Africa, and Southeast Asia.

World Vision also does amazing disaster relief work. They are also in the business of micro-loan financing for budding entrepreneurs in the developing world. Unknown to most people, World Vision has a great inner city ministry in the U.S. as well. http://www.worldvision.org/

World Relief is another incredible global community development organization which has its hands in a wide range of terribly important social justice issues ranging from disaster relief, to anti-trafficking, to health and education. They often get overlooked by the more visible presence of World Vision, but they have actually been at it even longer. This is their vision:

We practice principles of transformational development to empower local churches in the United States and around the world so they can serve the vulnerable in their communities. With initiatives in education, health, child development, agriculture, food security, anti-trafficking, immigrant services, micro-enterprise, disaster response and refugee resettlement, we work holistically with the local church to stand for the sick, the widow, the orphan, the alien, the displaced, the devastated, the marginalized, and the disenfranchised.

World Relief is especially on the frontlines of comprehensive immigration reform in the United States.

http://worldrelief.org/

My favorite branch of World Relief is in Garden Grove, CA, and it's led by my close friend, Glen Peterson. http://worldreliefgardengrove.org/

*Clean Water*

1 billion people on planet earth don't have clean water. 3.575 million people die each year from water-related diseases, and a child dies from water-born illness every 8 seconds. Clean water is one of the biggest

social justice issues of our time.[3]    A number of good Christian organizations have stepped up to the plate to address this compelling social justice issue of our time.   Once again, here are a few for your consideration:

Charity: Water    http://www.charitywater.org/

The Water Project:    http://thewaterproject.org/

World Vision:

http://donate.worldvision.org/OA_HTML/xxwv2ibeCCtpSct DspRte.jsp?section=10373

World Relief: http://worldrelief.org/page.aspx?pid=2479

*Hunger*

Despite the fact that the world produces enough food to feed every person on the planet, 925 million people suffer from hunger each year. 3.8 million children die each year from hunger-related causes every year.  Every 7 seconds a child dies from hunger.  There is no reason why this has to continue.[4]    Partner with these great organizations to help stop hunger:

World Vision    http://www.worldvision.org/

World Relief    http://worldrelief.org/

World Hunger Relief    http://worldhungerrelief.org/

Food For the Hungry    http://fh.org/

Christian Hunger Relief    http://freerice.com/

*AIDS and Other Preventable Diseases*

Millions of people die each year from highly-preventable diseases, and one billion people lack access to healthcare systems. AIDS caused 1.8 million deaths in 2009. This translates into almost 5,000 people everyday. HIV-AIDS has claimed the lives of 25 million people.

1.7 million people are killed by tuberculosis annually. 1.6 million people die from pneumococcal diseases. 780,000 individuals die from malaria.

The terrible tragedy is that most of these millions of deaths are preventable.[5] What are followers of Jesus going to do about it? These are several organizations that can help:


World Vision:  http://www.wvi.org/my/node/205

World Relief:  http://worldrelief.org/page.aspx?pid=1621

Pan African Christian Aids Network:  www.pacanet.net

Presbyterian Aids Network

> www.presbyterianmission.org/ministries/phewa/pres
> byterian-aids-network/

Cure:  www.cure.org/about

Mercy Ships    www.mercyships.org/

Cross International    www.crossinternational.org/

Giving of Life    https://givingoflife.com/


*Micro-Financing*

In my opinion, the most effective Christian community development work empowers indigenous leaders to rebuild their own communities.

Micro-financing is one of the most powerful tools to promote indigenous economic development. It gives small, micro-loans to entrepreneurs in developing communities who would otherwise not have the capital to start their own businesses. There are also great Christian orgs doing micro-financing and you can contact them to invest in these global "start-ups."

> For more information, see:
> World Vision        http://www.worldvisionmicro.org/fund-a-loan?utm_campaign=brand&utm_medium=paid-search&utm_source=google&utm_content=monetary-ask&utm_term=world%20vision%20microfinance
> World Relief      http://worldrelief.org/microfinance
> Hope International      http://www.hopeinternational.org/
> Peer Servants      http://www.peerservants.org/
> Five Talents      http://www.fivetalents.org/

*Fair Trade*

The goal of the fair trade movement is to create sustainable economic opportunities for artisans and small-scale agricultural producers of the developing world by selling their products in North America at a fair price. I.e.,the opposite business model of Wal-Mart. Unknown to most people, the fair trade movement has Christian roots. It was established by Mennonite Edna Ruth Byler in 1946. Her efforts led to the development of an organization called Ten Thousand Villages. It's still an official ministry of the Mennonite Central Committee, and the best in the world at what it does: www.tenthousandvillages.com/

*Human Trafficking: Not for Sale, International Justice Mission, El Pozo de Vida (The Well of Life), and Freedom and Fashion.*

There are 30 million slaves in the world. This is more than in any other time in human history. 1.2 million children are trafficked each year. 43% of human slaves are used for forced commercial sexual exploitation. 32% are used for forced economic exploitation. Between 14,000 and 17,500 people are trafficked into the United State each year. Large numbers of undocumented immigrants in the United States are categorized by the United Nations as slaves.

Numerous Christian organizations have joined the international fight against human trafficking. Here are just a few:

Not For Sale Campaign: Put simply, Not For Sale is one of the largest anti-slavery movements in the world. They have an amazing amount of resources for those who are interested in helping to end human trafficking. http://www.notforsalecampaign.org/

The International Justice Mission (IJM): IJM is an incredible global organization which rescues hundreds of people from slavery each year from around the world. IJM was founded by Gary Haugen who formerly served as Officer in Charge of the United Nation's genocide investigation in Rwanda.

As stated on their website: "IJM is a human rights agency that secures justice for victims of slavery, sexual exploitation and other forms of violent oppression. IJM lawyers, investigators and aftercare professionals work with local governments to ensure victim rescue, to prosecute perpetrators and to strengthen the community and civic

factors that promote functioning public justice systems."
http://www.ijm.org/

El Pozo de Vida, A.C. (The Well of Life) fights for the eradication of modern-day slavery and human trafficking through raising awareness, participation in advocacy for victims, and rescue and rehabilitation. El Pozo has a rescue home located in Mexico City, Mexico, where underage victims of sexual exploitation enter a restoration and rehabilitation program, and receive education, medical attention and psychological care. It's also led by two of our close friends. http://www.elpozodevida.org.mx/

Freedom and Fashion (FnF) is a human-trafficking awareness organization founded by one of our former students, Bonnie Kim. FnF raises public awareness about global slavery through a creative fusion of the fashion industry and the fair trade movement. FnF sponsors fashion shows featuring fair trade products and vendors. We are very proud of you, Bonnie! http://freedomandfashion.com/

World Vision and World Relief are also actively involved in the fight against human slavery. Aren't they amazing orgs! http://www.worldvision.org/content.nsf/learn/globalissues-child-trafficking

http://worldrelief.org/human-trafficking


*Undocumented Immigrant Advocacy: World Relief, Christians for Comprehensive Immigration Reform, and Loving the Stranger Network*

As this book has tried to highlight, justice for undocumented immigrants is one of the most important civil rights issues of our time.

Some have even said that it is as important today as the issue of slavery was 150 years ago. Here are some Christian groups on the forefront of this fight:

World Relief http://worldrelief.org/advocate

It is important to note that World Relief has been at the forefront of organizing evangelical Christian organizations to take a stand against the marginalization and exploitation of undocumented immigrants in the United States. It has also been at the cutting edge of advocacy for comprehensive immigration reform.

Evangelical Immigration Table: as discussed in chapter 3, this group consists of a broad coalition of evangelical churches and organizations who are committed to humane and compassionate comprehensive immigration reform.
http://evangelicalimmigrationtable.com/)

The Evangelical Immigration Table has also sponsored a nationwide effort to pray for immigration reform: http://g92.org/pray4reform/, and a public awareness campaign called the "I Was A Stranger Challenge":
http://evangelicalimmigrationtable.com/iwasastranger/

To get connected with young evangelicals who are committed to advocacy on behalf of the undocumented immigrant community, see: http://g92.org/

Christians for Comprehensive Immigration Reform (CCIR) is comprised of people who do just what its name says: Christians advocating for immigrant rights and comprehensive immigration reform on a national level in the United States. CCIR is a campaign of Sojourners. http://faithandimmigration.org

For those of us on the west coast, another immigrant advocacy group is the Loving the Stranger Network. This organization was founded by Glen Peterson and it's got a great blog and many resources for those interested in joining the fight for undocumented immigrant civil rights: http://lovingthestranger.blogspot.com/

*New Song Church and "Xealot"*

I would be remiss if I didn't give a shout-out to my "peeps" from the New Song family of churches. More than any other church that I know, the New Song churches uphold biblical justice as a core value of their congregations. Pastors Adam Edgerly and Cue Jean-Marie from New Song L.A. are my "brothas from another motha," and they have walked closely with me as I have endeavored to learn about God's heart for the poor over the past eight years. http://www.newsong.net/

Pastor Dave Gibbons, founder of the New Song family, has also spearheaded pioneering global community development projects through the "Xealot" organization. http://www.xealots.org/about-us/

*Seminaries and Academic Institutions*

Are you looking to go to seminary or to become a pastor? Are you looking for a seminary dedicated to racial inclusion and community development? Here are a few for you to check out:

Institute for the Study of Asian American Christianity (ISAAC): http://www.isaacweb.org/

ISSAC (I love that acronym) is a pioneering organization founded and directed by my friend, Young Lee-Hertig. ISAAC spearheads what is basically Christian Asian American Studies. As part of the Asian American civil rights movement, ISAAC was birthed through racial challenge in the field of seminary education. They host an annual symposium and also have a journal called, *SANACS (Society of Asian North American Christian Studies)*. Of all the institutions cited in this section, ISAAC is my favorite!

SCUPE: http://scupe.org/about-scupe/

> SCUPE is a consortium of seminaries devoted to urban renewal and racial equity.

Fuller Theological Seminary: http://www.fuller.edu/

> Fuller has a special Youth Institute for urban workers: http://www.fulleryouthinstitute.org/

> Fuller also has a unique program in Christian "ethics." Ethics in this context is another word for exploring social justice issues from a biblical perspective: http://www.fuller.edu/christianethics/. After 8 years of being a professor, I've now begun a graduate degree program in theology at Fuller!

Bakke Graduate University: http://www.bgu.edu/

BGU was founded by Christian community development pioneer, Ray Bakke. It offers an amazing array of graduate degrees focused upon community development and global justice.

Azusa Pacific University:

Located in Azusa, California, APU has master's programs in Transformational Urban Leadership: http://www.apu.edu/clas/globalstudies/urbanleadership/admission/

And, Pastoral Studies with an emphasis in Urban Studies:

http://www.apu.edu/theology/graduate/maps/urbanstudies/

If you're an undergrad, APU also has a special program in urban ministry called, "Los Angeles Term": http://www.apu.edu/laterm/

They also have an international version called, "Global Learning Term": http://www.apu.edu/studyabroad/programs/global/

Justice and Spirituality in Education (JSE) Conference and Journal: http://education.biola.edu/jseconf/

The JSE Conference and Journal were founded by my friend and Chicano Professor, Fred Ramirez. He's "down." As its name implies, the conference and journal are concerned with the intersection of justice, spirituality, and education. Check em' out!

North Park University:

Center for Youth Ministry Studies

Are you looking for an awesome place to prepare for a career in urban youth ministry in the Midwest? Check this program out!

http://www.northpark.edu/Centers/Center-for-Youth-Ministry-Studies

Kilns College: http://education.biola.edu/jseconf/

Located in Bend, Oregon, Kilns College is offering a master's degree in Social Justice.

http://www.kilnscollege.org/events/Master_of_Arts_Degree_in_Social_Justice

New York Theological Seminary:

The Micah Institute, at NYTS - http://nyts.edu/the-micah-institute/

"Inspired by the Hebrew prophet Micah's call to act justly, love mercy and walk humbly with God, we seek to inspire and educate faith leaders to fight poverty and injustice…"

*Law: Christian Legal Society, Mission First, Christian Legal Aid Foundation of Los Angeles, and I wish there were more*

A huge "justice gap" exists in the United States.[6]   Thousands of valid legal claims of the poor go unheard every year because no lawyer is willing to take their case.   For example, 1 of every 3 valid legal claims of the poor in California goes unheard because there is no one to take their case.   This has led to a two-tiered legal justice system in the United States:  one for the rich who can afford attorneys; and another for the poor who cannot.

Fortunately, there are a growing number of Christian public interest law firms in the United States!   Many have heard the call of Proverbs 31 to speak up for those who cannot speak for themselves and for the rights of all who are destitute.   But we still need many more! At the forefront of this movement to establish faith-based legal aid law firms and clinics is the Christian Legal Society.

Founded in 1961, the Christian Legal Society is a national network of Christian attorneys, judges, and paralegals. As part of their "Legal Aid Ministry," hundreds of thousands of hours have been donated by legal professionals to serve low-income clients in the past decade. Their mission statement reads:

CLS is a membership organization of Christian attorneys, judges, paralegals, law students, and other legal professionals dedicated to serving Jesus Christ through the practice of law, defense of religious freedom, and provision of legal aid to the needy. http://www.clsnet.org/

For a directory of Christian public interest clinics in the United States which was put together by the Christian Legal Society, see: www.clsnet.com/document.doc?id=43

Here's a sampling a few more for you to explore:

Mission First:    founded in Jackson, Mississippi in 2006, Mission First provides pro-bono legal services for the "working poor"—those who make "too much" money to qualify for traditional legal aid services, but not enough to afford an attorney on their own.  I love their website!  Check it out and support them and get inspired to start      your      own      legal      aid      nonprofit! http://www.missionfirst.org/legalaid

Christian Legal Clinics of Philadelphia:    This Christian legal organization has a very unique approach.    They partner with community-based ministries such as the Salvation Army and house their legal clinics on site!  This ensures that their clients receive access to a holistic range of services, not just the legal.  Very smart!  Drawing upon this model they have set up two clinics in the poorest sections of Philly.  Great job! http://www.clcphila.org/wp/

The Christian Legal Aid Foundation of Los Angeles (CLAF-LA) is one of the (unfortunately) few Christian non-profit legal services organizations serving the poor in California. They do great work, but unfortunately operate on a shoe-strong budget.  To donate your time or resources to this fine ministry see their website:  www.cla-la.org/cla-la-org/

>And a few more…
>Christian Legal Aid Office of Southern California:
>http://www.christianlegalaidoffice.com/
>Legal Aid Ministries (Dallas Texas):
>http://legalaidministries.com/
>New Mexico Christian Legal Aid:
>http://nmchristianlegalaid.org/
>Compassionate Counsel of Tennesse:
>http://compassionatecounsel.org/
>Twin Cities Christian Legal Aid:
>http://www.tccla.org/

*Christian Students of Conscience:  Join our Virtual Community, Launch a Jesus for Revolutionaries Action Group, or Start a Branch of CSC!*

In closing, I can't help but mention our own non-profit organization, Christian Students of Conscience (CSC).  CSC networks, trains, and mobilizes college and university students around issues of urban, racial, and global justice from a Christian perspective.  CSC also seeks to provide a Christian community for college and university students who love Jesus but who might not feel comfortable in traditional campus ministries.  Everything I've talked about in this book has been a product of our ministry with CSC over the past 8 years. This book could also be titled, simply, *CSC*.

Please join our CSC/Jesus for Revolutionaries virtual community on the internet, Facebook, and Twitter!

Our website and blog: www.jesusforrevolutionaries.org/

You can also like Christian Students of Conscience on Facebook, or,

Join our Christian Students of Conscience Group on Facebook!

Follow me on Twitter: @ProfeChaoRomero

Another opportunity for you to get involved would be to **launch a "Jesus For Revolutionaries" Praxis Group in your community!** If you go to our website (www.jesusforrevolutionaries.org/) you'll find a complete, and free, packet of study guide materials. All you have to do is call your friends, order some coffee, and you're ready to go! We hope that these "Jesus for Revolutionaries" studies can pop up all over the world and *ignite an organic and grass-roots Jesus Revolution!*

Finally, you can also **start a branch of CSC at your local college campus!** If you would be interested in launching a branch of CSC, please contact us: jesusforrevolutionaries@gmail.com. We would be thrilled to work with you to help make this happen! http://www.jesusforrevolutionaries.org/

I hope that this brief overview has shown that there are many modern-day *Revolutionaries* who passionately aspire to live out Jesus' heart for justice. I especially hope that their example might inspire you to get involved with one of the many wonderful Christian organizations in the world who are authentically *seeking the Jesus, the Ultimate Revolutionary*.

*PraXis*

1.    Which of these Christian social justice organizations stood out to you? Why?

2.    Which of these organizations would you like to get involved with? Get in touch with them today!

3.    One of the most transformative experiences for me was going to a national conference of the CCDA (Christian Community Development Association). It opened my eyes to a whole new world of Christian social justice that I didn't even know existed. Give a call to a few friends and plan a trip to the next one! http://www.ccda.org/

4.    Go check out the Justice Conference! http://thejusticeconference.com/

# 17    Join the Revolution!

This final chapter is really the most important of this whole book because it is a call to action.   This chapter asks you to search your heart, reflect, and ask yourself *one simple question*: *Will you join the Revolution?*

Many of us have seen "altar calls."  A pastor or evangelist shares a meaningful spiritual message and then invites his or her listeners to respond by walking down the aisle to the front of the church as a sign of commitment.  What most people don't know is that the altar call was originally a social justice call to action!  During the abolition/anti-slavery movement in the United States, Christians were at the forefront.  Many of them in fact, were pastors.

Christian abolitionists used the altar call as a way of recruiting people to fight for the abolition of slavery!  Christian pastors would preach spiritual messages about following Jesus and the evils of slavery, and then guess what they would do?  They would invite people to walk down to the altar at the front of the church and pledge themselves to follow God and fight against slavery!  Isn't that amazing!  How far we've strayed from these historical roots!

That's the point of this final chapter.  *Will you walk with me now down the aisle to the metaphorical altar at the front of the church and commit yourself to following Jesus and joining His revolution of justice?*

*Jesus invites you to come, follow him, and join the Revolution He began 2,000 years ago.*

To join, Jesus asks nothing from you, but that you surrender your life to Him.

You don't have to do anything to earn His love and favor. His love is a pure gift.

There's nothing that you can do or not do to make Jesus love you more; and there's nothing you can do or not do to make Jesus love you less.

You see, Jesus launched His Revolution by giving His life for you and me, and the whole world. He died on the cross to pay the price for our sins and to make the whole world new. To show that He really means what He says, He rose again on the third day.

On the cross He paid the price for every sin of injustice and racism that has ever been or ever will be. He took it all upon Himself because *His plan is* to *make the world new—free of injustice and bigotry and racism of every kind.* His plan is also to make the world free of all the other types of things we do to ourselves and one another which hurts us, causes us pain, destroys our families and friendships, and, ultimately, separates us from God. *Jesus came to make the whole world new.*

The Revolution begins for each of us when we surrender our life to Jesus. Like the father of the prodigal son story, He forgives us of all our sins, no matter how heinous and no matter how much guilt we have been carrying because of them. Jesus wipes the slate clean and gives us "beauty for ashes" because He already dealt with our sins on the cross, *once and for all.*

Jesus then gives us a new heart and breathes life into our souls. In Him, we find true *life* and a peace which transcends human understanding.

The next step is to follow Him the rest of our lives as His apprentices, and as God's beloved children. During the life-long journey as His apprentices, He heals us of the deep emotional pains and hurts which go unseen to all but those who know us best, and which torment us when we think no one else is looking. Jesus sees. He desires to bring deep healing and transformation to our wounded souls.

As we journey as His apprentices, Jesus also frees us from the sins and addictions which have held us prisoner. Although He loves us just as we are, and we do not have to do anything to gain his approval, He loves us too much to leave us unchanged.

The road to healing and freedom is a life-long process, but Jesus promises to direct our steps and to always be with us. His desire is to also bring other revolutionaries alongside us who can help carry the load. The revolutionary life is not a solitary endeavor.

The more and more we journey with Him as His students and apprentices, the more we find life. The Bible calls this *"eternal life."* Eternal life is often incorrectly described as something we only experience after we pass from this earth. *Eternal life is knowing Jesus. Now, and forever.* For those of us who have the privilege of knowing Jesus now, Heaven is simply the eternal (and perfect) continuation of the life we have already known in Jesus while here on earth. Moreover, as followers of Jesus, our ultimate hope is that when He returns again, all will be made new and Heaven and Earth will be made one. All things will then be restored to God's glorious intent. In the words of Archbishop Oscar Romero:

"God's reign is already present on our earth in mystery.
When the Lord comes, it will be brought to perfection.
That is the hope that inspires Christians.
We know that every effort to better society,
especially when injustice and sin are so ingrained,
is an effort that God blesses,
that God wants,
that God demands of us."

As stated so beautifully by Bishop Romero, once we join Jesus, He *sends us out to be his Revolutionaries.* He sends us out to love the poor, the immigrant, and the disenfranchised of society on his behalf. This is really the whole point of this book. As St. Augustine and Mother Theresa said, we learn to see Jesus in the poor. More than that, *we learn to love Jesus in the poor.*

Inspired and empowered by our Savior, we love the poor through God-inspired acts of mercy and compassion. We serve alongside them and empower them to rebuild and become indigenous leaders of their own communities. We help to meet basic physical needs such as food, housing, and we medical care, but we also seek to change the sinful human structures and systems which oppress the poor and reinforce social inequalities of every kind.

As we share the love of Christ to the poor, we also introduce Him to those who may not already know Him. In a spirit of deepest humility, we share with them about the Savior who has transformed us and given us life. We pray that they might also come to know God's amazing love and peace. Jesus is too beautiful and amazing to keep to ourselves. If you really know Jesus, you can't help but share.

*This is Jesus' Revolution. Would you like to join?*

If your desire is to follow Jesus and join His Revolution, all you have to do is ask. Find a quiet place. Surrender your life to Him. Thank Him for giving His life for you on the cross. Thank Him for His unconditional love. Follow Him all the days of your life. Make Him your Lord and King. Like a Star Wars padawan, like Yoda and Luke Skywalker, become His apprentice. That's how the Revolution begins...

The next step is to find a community of fellow Revolutionaries that can help support you in your personal journey with Jesus. Find a church filled with Revolutionaries who are head over heals in love with Jesus and who band together to help each other live out the Christian life. It's also very important to find a church that treasures and teaches from the ultimate revolutionary manual--the Bible.

In the appendix which follows, we've listed some good books and resources which we hope will also help you grow in your new relationship with Jesus. We've also included more resources on our website: www.jesusforrevolutionaries.org/

Feel free to contact us by email, jesusforrevolutionaries@gmail.com and let us know if there is any way that we can help support you on your new spiritual journey.

*"I want to learn more."*

Do these words describe you? Has your interest in Christianity been piqued by what you have read in this book, but you desire to learn more before making any type of commitment to join Jesus and His Revolution? I have a challenge for you.

Find a quiet place. Talk with God. Be honest with Him about your questions and concerns. Ask Him to reveal Himself to you. Take the leap of faith. You might be surprised by what God will show you...

To assist you in the further exploration of the Christian faith, we have included some resources in Appendix II which may help in addressing some of the questions you might have. We also have other resources on our website: www.jesusforrevolutionaries.org/.

You can always drop us an email, too, and we'd be glad to speak with you. Even better, have coffee with a friend who is also a follower of Jesus. I'm sure that she or he would be glad to speak with you about what it means to follow Jesus and about the Christian life.


*Launch a "Jesus for Revolutionaries" Praxis Group*

The whole goal of this book is to launch an organic, grass-roots, viral movement of Christian social justice in the United States and around the world! One way for this happen is for readers like you to start Jesus For Revolutionaries Praxis Groups all over the place! If you're interested in helping us to launch a mini-revolution in your community, go to our CSC website and you'll find a complete, and free, packet of study guide materials—all that you need to light a spark of Jesus revolution! www.jesusforrevolutionaries.org/

*Que viva la revolución!*

*Start a Chapter of "Christian Students of Conscience"*

Are you a college student? As discussed in the previous chapter, my wife and I began a ministry called "Christian Students of Conscience" to train and mobilize college students around issues of justice and race from a Christian perspective. A further goal of CSC is to provide a community for those students who are passionate about issues of justice but who might not feel completely at home within traditional campus organizations. Would you like to start a local branch of CSC at a college or university campus in the United States or abroad? We would love to partner with you and show you how you can launch a CSC at a college or university near you! Drop us an email and we can talk more: jesusforrevolutionaries@gmail.com.

*Thank you*

Finally, I would like to say, "thanks" for taking the time to read this book.   I know that there were many other things you could have chosen to do with your time.  It has been a privilege to share with you about the things that God has taught me, and is still teaching me. I pray that this book might help people to know Jesus better.

      Robert Chao Romero

      Los Angeles

      October 5, 2013

# Appendix I: A Faith and Justice Manifesto

The vision of Christian Students of Conscience is to launch Christ-centered movements of justice and racial reconciliation at colleges and universities throughout the United States, and abroad. To this end, CSC is dedicated to the following specific goals: (1) Networking Christian students of conscience throughout the world to advocate for the important justice issues of our time; (2) training and mobilizing students around issues of poverty, justice, and race from a faith-rooted, biblical perspective; (3) creating a community of faith for students who are passionate about issues of race and justice; and, (4) promoting Christian community development among the poor of the United States and abroad.

As Christian Students of Conscience we believe:

> Every human being is made equally in the image and likeness of God (Genesis 1: 27).

> By God's design, we each uniquely reflect the image of God in terms of our distinct cultural backgrounds, gender, and personal gifts, talents, and abilities (Revelation 21: 26. Genesis 1: 27. Psalm 8: 3-5).

> This distinct image of God is marred within each of us because of sin (Romans 5: 12-13).

Jesus willingly gave His life and rose again to bring us back into personal relationship with Himself, to restore the distinct image of God within each of us, and to make the whole world new (1 Corinthians 15: 21-22. Romans 5: 15-19. 2 Corinthians 3: 18. Revelation 21:5. Colossians 1: 15-20. Isaiah 9:6-7).

Jesus died not only for our personal sins, but also for the structural and systemic sins of our society which perpetuate poverty, racism, sexism, classism, and injustice of every kind (Romans 13: 8-10).

Poverty exists because we fail to love our neighbors as ourselves.

Racism exists because we fail to love our neighbors as ourselves.

Sexism exists because we fail to love our neighbors as ourselves.

Injustice exists because we fail to love our neighbors as ourselves.

Jesus is a God of justice and compassion (Matthew 25: 31-46. James 5:1-6. Psalm 11:7).

He loves the poor (Psalm 140: 12. 1 Samuel 2: 8).

He loves immigrants (Deuteronomy 10: 18. Psalm 146: 9. Exodus 22: 21).

He loves all those that are marginalized and dispossessed by society.

Jesus identifies so closely with the poor that He teaches that our response to them is a barometer of our love for Him (Matthew 25: 31-46).

As followers of Jesus we are called to obey all of His commandments and teachings (John 14: 23-24).

This includes loving immigrants, the poor, and the dispossessed of society (Leviticus 19: 33-34. Deuteronomy 15: 11).

This also involves advocating on their behalf (Proverbs 31: 8-9).

The vision of CSC is to launch Christ-centered movements of justice and racial reconciliation at UCLA and at colleges and universities throughout the United States and abroad.

CSC invites Christ-followers of every denominational background to join us in launching and participating in these movements of justice and racial reconciliation.

CSC also welcomes those who care about issues of justice and race and who are curious about learning more about God's heart for justice and the poor, and about exploring a personal relationship with Jesus.

We believe that the Bible is the inspired Word of God, and therefore without error. As such, it is our guide for faith, practice, and all the activities of CSC (2 Timothy 3: 16-17).

# Appendix II: More Resources for the Budding Revolutionary—Books, Films, and Immigration

## Books on Justice and Community Development:

*A Theology as Big as the City.* Ray Bakke

*Not For Sale: The Return of the Global Slave Trade—and How We Can Fight It.* David Batstone

*Practical Justice: Living off-Center in a Self-Centered World.* Kevin Blue

*Tattoos on the Heart: The Power of Boundless Compassion,* Father Gregory Boyle (Homeboy Industries)

*Choose Love Not Power: How to Right the World's Wrongs From A Place of Weakness.* Tony Campolo

*Following Jesus Without Embarrassing God.* Tony Campolo

*The God of Intimacy and Action: Reconnecting Ancient Spiritual Practices, Evangelism, and Justice.* Tony Campolo & Mary Albert Darling

*Red Letter Christians: A Citizen's Guide to Faith and Politics.* Tony Campolo

*The Irresistible Revolution.* Shane Claiborne

*The Red Letter Revolution: What If Jesus Really Meant What He Said?* Shane Claiborne and Tony Campolo

*United By Faith: The Multiracial Congregation as An Answer to the Problem of Race.* Curtiss Paul DeYoung, Michael Emerson, et al.

*Plunge2Poverty: An Intensive Poverty Simulation Experience.* Jimmy and Janet Dorrell

*Divided By Faith: Evangelical Religion and the Problem of Race in America.* Michael Emerson and Christian Smith

*Hotel on the Corner of Bitter and Sweet.* Jamie Ford

*The Pedagogy of the Oppressed.* Paulo Freire

*The Gospel of Cesar Chavez.* Mario T. Garcia

*Manana: Christian Theology from a Hispanic Perspective.* Justo Gonzalez

*The Story of Christianity, Volume 1: The Early Church to the Dawn of the Reformation (Story of Christianity).* Justo L. Gonzalez

*The Story of Christianity, Vol. 2: The Reformation to the Present Day.* Justo L. Gonzalez

*Evangelicalism and Social Responsibility.* Vernon Grounds. Available as a free download: http://denverseminary.edu.s3.amazonaws.com/uploaded/e/0e372783 _evangelicalism-and-social-responsibility.pdf

*An' push da wind down: A play in two acts.* Lisa Harper

*Evangelical Does Not Equal Republican or Democrat.* Lisa Sharon Harper

*Left, Right & Christ: Evangelical Faith in Politics.* Lisa Sharon Harper & D.C. Innes

*Being White: Finding Our Place in a Multiethnic World.* Paula Harris and Doug Schaupp

*The Good News About Injustice.* Gary Haugen

*Mirrored Reflections: Reframing Biblical Characters.* Young Lee Hertig and Chloe Sun (Ground-breaking book about theology from an Asian American female perspective)

*Heaven Has a Ghetto: The Missiological Gospel & Theology of Tupac Amaru Shakur.* Daniel White Hodge.

*The Soul of Hip Hop: Rims, Timbs & Cultural Theology.* Daniel White Hodge.

*The Secret Life of Bees.* Sue Monk Kidd

*Letter from A Birmingham Jail.* Rev. Martin Luther King, Jr.

*The Dangerous Act of Worship: Living God's Call to Justice.* Mark Labberton

*To Kill A Mockingbird.* Harper Lee

*A Credible Witness.* Brenda Salter McNeil

*The Heart of Racial Justice.* Brenda Salter McNeil

*Protestant Hispanics Serving the Community: A Research Project Funded by the Pew Charitable Trusts.* Michael Mata and Karen Hemmer Tarbell

*Enrique's Journey: The Story of a Boy's Dangerous Odyssey to Reunite with His Mother.* Sonia Nazario. See also the YA version adapted for young readers!

*A Framework for Understanding Poverty.* Ruby Payne

*Beyond Charity: The Call to Christian Community Development.* John Perkins

*With Justice for All.* John Perkins

*More Than Equals: Racial Healing for the Sake of the Gospel.* Spencer Perkins & Chris Rice

*Putting Faith First: Traditions and Innovations in Organizing within Religious Communities*

http://dornsife.usc.edu/pere/publications/index.cfm

*Christians at the Border: Immigration, the Church, and the Bible.* M. Daniel Carroll R.

*Disunity in Christ.* Christena Cleveland

*Letters to A Mixed Race Son.* Frank E. Robinson, Jr.

*The Violence of Love.* Archbishop Oscar Romero. Free e-book: http://www.plough.com/en/ebooks/uv/violence-of-love

Clarence Shuler. *Winning the Race to Unity: Is Racial Reconciliation Really Working?*

*Rich Christians in an Age of Hunger.* Ronald J. Sider

*Welcoming the Stranger: Justice, Compassion & Truth in the Immigration Debate,* Matthew Soerens & Jenny Hwang

*Black Rednecks and White Liberals.* Thomas Sowell

*The Hole in Our Gospel: What Does God Expect of Us? The Answer that Changed My Life and Just Might Change the World.* Richard Stearns

*The Help.* Kathryn Stockett

*Mobilizing Hope: Faith-Inspired Activism for a Post-Civil Rights Generation.* Adam Taylor

*Jesus & the Hip-Hop Prophets: Spiritual Insights from Lauryn Hill and 2Pac,* John Teter and Alex Gee

*Underground Undergrads: UCLA Undocumented Immigrant Students Speak Out*

*Undocumented and Unafraid: Tam Tran, Cinthya Felix, and the Immigrant Youth Movement*

*Across the Wire: Life and Hard Times on the Mexican Border.* Luis Urrea

*The Great Awakening: Reviving Faith & Politics in a Post-Religious Right America.* Jim Wallis

*God's Politics: Why the Right Gets it Wrong and the Left Doesn't Get It.* Jim Wallis

*Pursuing Justice: The Call to Live & Die for Bigger Things.* Ken Wytsma


## Books about Life-Calling and Living the Christian Life

*Experiencing God: Knowing and Doing the Will of God* (Workbook), Henry Blackaby and Claude King

*The Sacred Romance.* John Eldridge

*Celebration of Discipline: The Path to Spiritual Growth.* Richard J. Foster

*Abba's Child.* Brennan Manning

*The Ragamuffin Gospel.* Brennan Manning

*Seizing Your Divine Moment.* Erwin McManus

*Uprising: A Revolution of the Soul.* Erwin McManus

*Living on Purpose: Finding God's Best for Your Life*, Christine and Tom Sine

*The Divine Conspiracy: Rediscovering Our Hidden Life in God.* Dallas Willard

*Renovation of the Heart: Putting On the Character or Christ.* Dallas Willard

*The Spirit of the Disciplines: Understanding How God Changes Lives.* Dallas Willard

*Church: Why Bother?* Philip Yancey

*Disappointment with God.* Philip Yancey

*Prayer: Does It Make Any Difference?* Philip Yancey

*What's So Amazing About Grace?* Philip Yancey


## Books About Emotional Healing

*Boundaries: How to Have that Difficult Conversation you've been Avoiding.* Henry Cloud & John Townsend

*Changes that Heal.* Henry Cloud

*How People Grow: What the Bible Reveals About Personal Growth.* Henry Cloud and John Townsend

*Warrior in Pink: A Story of Cancer, Community, and the One Who Comforts.* Vivian Mabuni

*The Wounded Healer.* Henri Nouwen

*Following Jesus Without Dishonoring Your Parents.* Jeanette Yep. Peter Cha. Greg Jao. (A book for Asian American students)


## Films and Documentaries about Race and Social Justice

"58: The Film"    http://www.live58.org/about/58-the-film/

"A Better Life"

"Amazing Grace"

"American History X"

"Amistad"

"Another World Is Possible", Vol. 2, "Poverty," Shane Claiborne

"An Unfinished Dream" (AB-540 Student Experiences)

http://www.anunfinisheddream.com

"Bastards of the Party"

"The Butler"

"Chinatown"

"Compassion by Command" by Here's Life Inner City, C.C.C. Compassionbycommand.com

"The Constant Gardener"

"Crash"

"Do the Right Thing"

"El Norte"

"Eyes on the Prize"

"Freedom Riders"

"Fruitvale Station"

"Good Night and Good Luck"

"Harvest of Empire" "The Lives of Others"

"Made in L.A."

"Maria Full of Grace"

"The Mission"

"My Neighborhood"

"Papers"

"Romero"

"Salt of the Earth"

"A Soldier's Story"

"Stand and Deliver"

"A Time to Kill"

"To Kill A Mockingbird"

"Under the Same Moon"

"The Visitor"

"Walkout"

"Welcome to Shelbyville"

"Zoot Suit"

## More Immigration Resources

California Immigrant Policy Center  http://www.caimmigrant.org/

CHIRLA  http://www.chirla.org/

The Coalition for Humane Immigrant Rights of Los Angeles (CHIRLA) was formed in 1986 to advance the human and civil rights of immigrants and refugees in Los Angeles; promote harmonious multi-ethnic and multi-racial human relations; and through coalition-building, advocacy, community education and organizing, empower immigrants and their allies to build a more just society.

The Migration Policy Institute http://www.migrationpolicy.org

MPI provides analysis, development, and evaluation of migration and refugee policies at the local, national, and international levels.

National        Domestic        Workers        Alliance
http://www.domesticworkers.org/

NDWA is the nation's leading voice for an estimated 2.5 million domestic workers in the United States, most of whom are women.

The USC Center for the Study of Immigrant Integration http://csii.usc.edu/

Mission: to remake the narrative for understanding, and the dialogue for shaping, immigrant integration in America. Identifies and evaluates the mutual benefits of immigrant integration for the native-born and immigrants and to study the pace of the ongoing transformation in different locations, not only in the past and present but projected into the future.

Welcoming America   http://www.welcomingamerica.org/

National, grassroots-driven collaborative that works to promote mutual respect and cooperation between foreign-born and U.S.-born Americans.

# Appendix III: PraXis Groups and The 4-Part Study

The goal of Jesus for Revolutionaries is to launch a grass roots, Jesus-centered, social justice movement throughout the United States and abroad. Jesus for Revolutionaries is designed to be an introduction to Jesus for student activists, as well as an introduction to the world of Christian social justice.

Our main vehicle for accomplishing these goals, we hope, will be through small groups. Our prayer is that many will feel led to read Jesus for Revolutionaries together in community as part of small groups, or, *PraXis Groups*. "Praxis" is a term which refers to the intersection of theory and practice.

We've called our groups PraXis Groups—with a capital "X"--to refer to the intersection of theory, practice, and X-stianity. Many social justice groups already exist, but not many have Jesus at the Center.

To make it easier to launch PraXis Groups, we've put together a simple *4-Part Study*
which can be used as a way of reading through the book in community. Here it is:

## Part I: Student Stories from the Revolution

The goal of Part I is to address the historical misrepresentation of Christianity which has led many students to fall away from faith. This representation has led many to believe that Christianity is a racist, classist, and sexist religion.

For this session, pick a historic site of racial struggle in your city. For example, if you're in L.A., you could meet at the site of the Rodney King uprising, the Watts Rebellion, the Santa Anita Race Tracks (which were former Japanese internment camps), the garment district in downtown Los Angeles, Chinatown, or Olvera Street. Another option would be to visit the "Great Wall of Los Angeles." http://sparcinla.org/programs/the-great-wall-mural-los-angeles/

Read the Introduction and chapters 14 and 15. Discuss the "PraXis Questions" at the end of each chapter.

## Part II: God's Equal Protection Clause: The Biblical Basis for Social Justice

Did you know that there are more than 2,000 verses in the Bible which talk about God's love and concern for immigrants and the poor? The goal of Part II is to introduce the reader to these verses, and to put them in action through an over-night retreat and service project.

Go to the following website of the Christian Community Development Association: http://www.ccda.org/members/practitioners-partners. Identify a Christian Community Development practitioner or partner organization in your area. Contact them and ask if you can volunteer at their organization as part of an overnight retreat. I'm sure they'll have many ideas…

As part of the retreat, read Chapters 1 and 2. Discuss the PraXis Questions at the end of each chapter. You can also ask someone from your partner organization to give a talk to your group about a topic that is important to her/his heart.

Serve your partner organization!

## Part III: Race, Class, and Gender: A Biblical Framework for Diversity

The goal of Part III is to introduce readers to a biblical framework for understanding race, class, and gender diversity.

For this session, explore an ethnic enclave in your community. Walk around, enjoy a meal, take it in…

Read chapters 9-13. Discuss PraXis Questions.


## Part IV: Modern Day Revolutionaries

This session introduces readers to the world of Christian social justice and asks one simple question: Will you join the Revolution?

Pick a beautiful spot in nature—mountains, ocean, lake, etc. Go for a hike.

Read chapters 16-17. Discuss PraXis Questions.

How has God spoken to your heart?
What are your next steps—personally? As a group?

---------------------------

## *Optional Sessions*

In addition to, or in place of, any of the four previous studies, you can also choose from the following optional sessions.

## Optional Session I:  Jesus Was An Immigrant

The goal of this session is to introduce readers to what the Bible has to say about God's love and concern for immigrants.  A second goal is to apply this scriptural understanding to the issue of undocumented immigration in the United States today.

Visit an immigrant community in your city.  Walk around, take it in, grab a meal, and appreciate all that immigrants contribute to your city.

Read chapters 2-5.  Discuss the PraXis Questions at the end of each chapter.

## Optional Session II:  Jesus Invented Affirmative Action

Unknown to most people, Jesus "invented affirmative action."

The goal of this session is to explore the biblical basis for affirmative action, and to apply this framework to the contemporary policy issue of affirmative action in higher education.

Go to: http://www.healthycity.org/

Do research on the demographic characteristics of where you live and the surrounding communities.    Observe the disparities between neighborhoods. The "playing field" is not equal for all. This is why affirmative action is still necessary.

Read chapters 6, 7, and 10. Discuss the PraXis Questions.

## Optional Session III: Jesus and the Tea Party

A lot of people get turned off to Christianity because of the way some people confuse Jesus with partisan politics. Jesus is not the same as the Republican Party, the Democratic Party, the Tea Party, or any partisan politics.

The goal of this session is to disentangle Christianity, and Jesus, from the cords of partisan politics in America.

Search the internet and find some examples of people confusing Christianity with partisan politics. Unfortunately it's not too hard to find…

Read chapter 8. Discuss the PraXis Questions.

## Optional Session IV:  Gender

Some people get turned off to Christianity because of the way unbiblical patriarchy gets infused into some churches.  The goal of this session is to explore what the Bible really has to say about men, women, and gender.  Some key topics include:  men, women, and the image of God; the Virgin of Guadalupe; and female leadership in the church.

Read chapters 11 and 13.  Discuss the PraXis Questions.

Notes

## Chapter 1

[1] Richard Stearns, *The Hole in Our Gospel: What Does God Expect of Us? The Answer That Changed My Life and Might Just Change the World* (Nashville: Thomas Nelson, 2010), 22.

## Chapter 3

[1] http://reformimmigrationforamerica.org/. I came across this statistic on a sign from a student advocacy group at Loyola Marymount University in 2008 when I was doing a post-doctoral fellowship year with the Ford Foundation.

[2] Bill Ong Hing. 2006. *Deporting Our Souls: Values, Morality, and Immigration Policy.* New York: Cambridge University Press. 13-14.

[3] Jeffrey S. Passel and D'Vera Cohn. 2008. *Trends in Unauthorized Immigration: Undocumented Inflow Now Trails Legal Inflow."* Pew Hispanic Center.

[4] Adrian Florido. 2010. "11 Million and Growing: Breaking Down the Number of Undocumented Immigrants in the US." PRI'S, the World. "http://www.theworld.org/2013/05/11-million-and-growing-breaking-down-the-number-of-undocumented-immigrants-in-the-us/

[5] Jessica Vaughan. 2008. "Proposal to Axe Green Cards for Unskilled Workers Considered." Center for Immigration Studies. I'm not a fan of this organization, but this article did have these helpful statistics. http://www.cis.org/vaughan/green-cards-for-unskilled-workers

[6] Ibid.

## Chapter 4

[1] U.S. Immigration and Customs Enforcement website: http://www.ice.gov/about/overview/

[2] Nancy Lofholm. 2011. "Statistician Explores Deportations Since 9/11." *DenverPost.com* http://www.denverpost.com/news/ci_18920405

[3] Ibid; Elise Foley. 2013. Obama Deportation Toll Could Pass 2 Million at Current Rates." *The Huffington Post.* http://www.huffingtonpost.com/2013/01/31/obama-deportation_n_2594012.html

[4] The Children of the Camps Project. "Children of the Camps: Internment History. PBS. http://www.pbs.org/childofcamp/history/

5  ICE. "Secure Communities." http://www.ice.gov/secure_communities/

6 Kathleen Kingsbury. 2008. "Immigration: No Correlation With Crime." *Time U.S.* http://www.time.com/time/nation/article/0,8599,1717575,00.html

7 Julia Preston. 2008. "California: Study of Immigrants and Crime." *NY Times.* http://www.nytimes.com/2008/02/26/us/26brfs-STUDYOFIMMIG_BRF.html?_r=0

8  Aarti Kohli, Peter L. Markowitz, and Lisa Chavez. 2011. *Secure Communities By the Numbers: An Analysis of Demographics and Due Process.* The Chief Justice Earl Warren Institute of Law and Social Policy. University of California, Berkeley Law School.

9 9Deport Nation. 2011. "New Data: Secure Communities Still Sweeping Up Low-Level Offenders, Non-Criminals. *Deportation Nation.* http://www.deportationnation.org/2011/03/new-data-secure-communities-still-sweeping-up-low-level-offenders-non-criminals/

10 Ibid.

11Michael Hennessey. 2011. "Secure Communities Destroys Public Trust." *SF Gate.* http://www.sfgate.com/opinion/article/Secure-Communities-destroys-public-trust-2373213.php

12David Dayen. 2011. "Hundreds of Latinos Protest Record Deportations and Secure Communities Program in Los Angeles." *FDL News Desk.* http://news.firedoglake.com/2011/08/16/hundreds-of-latinos-protest-record-deportations-and-secure-communities-program-in-los-angeles/

13Kate Desormeau. 2011. "Immigration Dragnet Sweeps Up Domestic Violence Victims." ACLU. http://www.aclu.org/blog/content/immigration-dragnet-sweeps-domestic-violence-victims

Chapter 5

1 *Plyler v. Doe*, 457 U.S. 202 (1982). http://www.law.cornell.edu/supct/html/historics/USSC_CR_0457_0202_ZD.html

2  Educators for Fair Consideration (E4FC). "Fact Sheet: An Overview of College-Bound Undocumented Students." www.e4fc.org/images/Fact_Sheet.pdf

3 Michael A. Olivas  2012. "Undocumented Children 30 Years After Plyler." American Constitution Society. ACS Blog. http://www.acslaw.org/acsblog/undocumented-children-30-years-after-plyler

[4] E4FC. www.e4fc.org/images/Fact Sheet.pdf

[5] Ibid.

[6] Gabriela Madera and UCLA Dreamers. 2008. *Underground Undergrads: UCLA Undocumented Immigrant Students Speak Out*. UCLA Center for Labor Research and Education. http://books.labor.ucla.edu/p/55/

[7] Daisy Barrera. 2011. "Student commits suicide, letters reveal worries over immigration status." *ValleyCentral.com* http://www.valleycentral.com/news/story.aspx?id=690993#.UdIN9YXNMfE

[8] Manny Fernandez. 2011. "Disillusioned Young Immigrant Kills Himself, Starting an Emotional Debate." *NY Times*. http://www.nytimes.com/2011/12/11/us/joaquin-luna-jrs-suicide-touches-off-immigration-debate.html?pagewanted=all

Chapter 6

[1] Rob Bell. 2005. *Velvet Elvis: Repainting the Christian Faith*. New York: HarperCollins. 124-134.

[2] Ibid.

Chapter 7

[1] NAACP. "Fact Sheet: African Americans and Education."

[2] Teach For America. 2012. www.teachforamerica.org,

[3] Ibid.

[4] Erica Jade Lyons. 2009. "Educational Inequity." Senior Project. California Polytechnic University, San Luis Obispo. 17. http://digitalcommons.calpoly.edu/socssp/11

[5] Ibid., 1.

[6] Bryan Cordes and Gerald Miller. *Inequality of Education in the United States*. Rockhurst University. 6. cte.rockhurst.edu/s/945/images/editor_documents/content/.../cordes.pdf

[7] Lyons, "Educational Inequity," 2.

[8] Tara J. Yosso and Daniel G. Solorzano. 2006. "Leaks in the Chicana and Chicano Educational Pipeline." Latino Policy and Issues Brief, Number 13. UCLA Chicano Studies Research Center.

http://www.chicano.ucla.edu/publications/report-brief/leaks-chicana-and-chicano-educational-pipeline

9 NAACP. "Fact Sheet: African Americans and Education."

10   Rena Hawkins and Melissa Robinson. "US Schools Are More Segregated Now Than in the 1950's." Project Censored: The News That Didn't Make the News. http://www.projectcensored.org/top-stories/articles/2-us-schools-are-more-segregated-today-than-in-the-1950s-source/

11 *Gratz v. Bollinger,* 539 U.S. 244 (2003).   http://www.oyez.org/cases/2000-2009/2002/2002_02_516

12 *Grutter v. Bollinger,* 539 U.S. 306 (2003).   http://www.oyez.org/cases/2000-2009/2002/2002_02_241/

Chapter 8

1 For more on Prop 14, see: David B. Oppenheimer. 2010.  "California's Anti-Discrimination Legislation, Proposition 14, and the Constitutional Protection of Minority Rights: The Fiftieth Anniversary of the California Fair Employment and Housing Act." *Golden Gate University Law Review,* Vol. 40, pp. 117-127.  http://www.uccnrs.ucsb.edu/publications/californias-anti-discrimination-legislation-proposition-14-and-constitutional-protectio

2   Jason Pace. 2013. "The Legacy of Cesar Chavez and Marcos Munoz."    Illinois Coalition for Immigrant and Refugee Rights. http://icirr.org/content/legacy-cesar-chavez-and-marcos-munoz

3 Joseph A. Palermo. 2010. "Archbishop Oscar Romero: Thirty Years and Little Learned." The Blog. *The Huffington Post.* http://www.huffingtonpost.com/joseph-a-palermo/archbishop-oscar-romero-t_b_511399.html

4 Susan Gzesh. 2006.  "Central Americans and Asylum Policy in the Reagan Era." Migration Information Source: Fresh Thought, Authoritative Data, Global Reach. http://www.migrationinformation.org/feature/display.cfm?ID=384

5  Ronald Walters. University of Maryland. "UMD Experts." http://www.newsdesk.umd.edu/experts/experts_lists/Reagan/RR.htm

6 Joe Davidson. 2004. "Reagan:  A Contrary View."  Race& Ethnicity on NBCNews.com. http://www.nbcnews.com/id/5158315/ns/us_news-life/t/reagan-contrary-view/#.UdQ8N4XNMb0

7 *United States v. Paradise,* 480 U.S. 149 (1987). http://www.law.cornell.edu/supct/html/historics/USSC_CR_0480_0149_ZS.html

[8] Ayn Rand Institute. "Essentials of Objectivism."
http://www.aynrand.org/site/PageServer?pagename=objectivism_essentials

[9] I'm not alone on this point. The late Chuck Colson, founder of Prison Fellowship, also felt the same: Brian Doherty. 2011. "Chuck Colson Warns the Right: Ayn Rand Hated God." Reason.com: Free Minds and Free Markets.
http://reason.com/blog/2011/05/11/chuck-colson-warns-the-right-a

Chapter 9

[1] You can find this fine poem in, *Crossing Lines: Race and Mixed Race Across the Geohistorical Divide*. 2003. Ed. Marc Coronado, Rudy P. Guevarra, Jr., Jeffrey Moniz, and Laura Furlan Szanto. Multiethnic Student Outreach, University of California, Santa Barbara.

[2] United States Census Bureau. 2012. "2010 Census Shows Multiple-Race Population Grew Faster Than Single-Race Population."
"http://www.census.gov/newsroom/releases/archives/race/cb12-182.html

[3] Jennifer Lee. "A Post-Racial Society or a Diversity Paradox?" Russell Sage Foundation. http://www.russellsage.org/research/post-racial-society-or-diversity-paradox

[4] Robert Chao Romero and Kevin Escudero. 2012. "'Asian-Latinos' and the United States Census." *UCLA AAPI Nexus Journal*. Vol. 10, No. 2.

[5] Influenster. http://www.influenster.com/review/mambo-by-liz-claiborne-cologne

[5] Gloria Anzaldua. 1999. *Borderlands/La Frontera: The New Mestiza*. San Francisco: Aunt Lute Books.

Chapter 10

[1] Nancy McCarthy. 2007. "394 Million 'Justice Gap' Plagues Legal Services." CaliforniaProBono.org. http://www.californiaprobono.org/news/article.133525-394_million_justice_gap_plagues_legal_services

[2] United States Census Bureau. 2011. "Income, Poverty and Health Insurance Coverage in the United States: 2010."
"http://www.census.gov/newsroom/releases/archives/income_wealth/cb11-157.html

[3] Annie Lowrey. 2013. "Racial Wealth Gap Widened During Recession." *New York Times*. http://www.nytimes.com/2013/04/29/business/racial-wealth-gap-widened-during-recession.html?pagewanted=all

[4] Teach For America. "The Achievement Gap."
http://www.teachforamerica.org/achievement-gap

[5] Tara J. Yosso and Daniel G. Solórzano. 2006. "Leaks in the Chicana and Chicano Educational Pipeline." Latino Policy and Issues Brief, Number 13.
http://www.chicano.ucla.edu/publications/report-brief/leaks-chicana-and-chicano-educational-pipeline

[6] NAACP. 2009. "Fact Sheet: African Americans and Education."naacp.3cdn.net/e5524b7d7cf40a3578_2rm6bn7vr.pdf

[7] Sidney M. Wolfe, M.D. 2012. "50 Million Uninsured in the U.S. Equals 50,000+ Avoidable Deaths a Year." *Public Citizen.* http://www.citizen.org/Page.aspx?pid=5268

[8] Christine Lagorio. 2009. "Study: 1 In 4 Kids Go Without Health Care." CBS Evening News with Scott Pelley. http://www.cbsnews.com/8301-18563_162-2755159.html

[9] Agency for Healthcare Research and Quality. 2013. "Addressing Racial and Ethnic Disparities in Health Care."
http://www.ahrq.gov/research/findings/factsheets/minority/disparit/

[10] Philippa Strum. 2010. *Mendez v. Westminster: School Desegregation and Mexican-American Rights.* Lawrence: University of Kansas Press.

[10]Roberta H. Martinez. 2009. *Latinos in Pasadena.* Charleston: Arcadia Publishing.

[11] Robert Chao Romero and Luis Fernando Fernandez. 2012. "*Doss v. Bernal*: Ending Mexican Apartheid in Orange County." UCLA CSRC Research Report. No. 14.
www.chicano.ucla.edu/files/RR14.pdf

[12]Nicole Santa Cruz. 2012. "Black Family Reports Hate Crimes in Yorba Linda." *Los Angeles Times.* http://articles.latimes.com/2012/nov/21/local/la-me-1121-black-family-harass-20121121

[13] For an amazing spoken-word tribute to Trayvon, see:
http://www.upworthy.com/everyone-has-one-great-poem-inside-them-and-this-actor-just-nailed-his?g=3

Chapter 11

[1] N. Sue Van Sant Palmer. 2011. "Honoring Katie Finn Milleman—Speaker Traces History of Women's Rise in the Legal Profession During Award Ceremony." *The Iowa Lawyer.* http://digital.turn-page.com/issue/40668/19

2 For more on the Junia controversy, see: Allison Quient. "Junia: Outstanding Among the Apostles." *Arise* E-Newsletter. Christians for Biblical Equality. http://www.cbeinternational.org/?q=content/2013-03-21-junia-outstanding-among-apostles-arise-e-newsletter

3 Michael Duricy. The Marian Library/International Marian Research Institute. "Our Lady of Guadalupe." http://campus.udayton.edu/mary/meditations/guadalupe.html

Chapter 14

1 Aime Cesaire. 1955. *Discourse on Colonialism.*

2 *The Guardian.* 2012. "Was colonialism to blame for the spread of HIV in Africa?" http://www.guardian.co.uk/society/shortcuts/2012/mar/04/was-colonialism-responsible-spread-hiv

3 Thomas M. Whitmore. 1991. "A Simulation of the Sixteenth-Century Population Collapse in the Basin of Mexico." *Annals of the Association of American Geographers,* Volume 81, Issue 3, 464–487.

4 Guenter Lewy. 2007. "Were American Indians the Victims of Genocide?" George Mason University's History News Network. http://hnn.us/articles/7302.html

5 Paul Foos. 2002. *A Short, Offhand Killing Affair: Soldiers and Social Conflict during the Mexican-American War.* Chapel Hill: The University of North Carolina Press.

6 Ibid.

7 Rodolfo F. Acuna. 2010. *Occupied America: A History of Chicanos.* New Jersey: Pearson.

8 Alexander Saxton. 1971. *The Indispensable Enemy: Labor and the Anti-Chinese Movement in California.* Berkeley: The University of California Press.

Chapter 15

1 Las Casas has been rightly criticized for his support of African slavery as an alternative to the enslavement of indigenous Mexicans. This was a profound flaw. On his death bed, however, he did recant his support for African slavery.

2 Bartolome de Las Casas. *History of the Indies.* As cited in, Kevin Reilly, ed. *Worlds of History* (Boston, 1999), 504-505. https://www2.stetson.edu/secure/history/hy10430/montesinos.html

3 For more on Las Casas, see the following website dedicated to his life and legacy: http://www.lascasas.org/

259

[4] Henry Chadwick. 1993. *The Early Church.* Penguin.

[5] Ibid.

[6] Eberhard Arnold. 1972. *The Early Christians: A Sourcebook on the Witness of the Early Church.* Grand Rapids: Baker Book House.

[7] Ibid., "Letter to Diognetus 10."

[8] Ibid., Aristides, "Apology;" "About 137 A.D."

[9] Ibid., Justin, "First Apology 14."

[10] "Didache: The Teaching of the Twelve Apostles." Chapter 3. Trans. Roberts-Donaldson. http://www.earlychristianwritings.com/text/didache-roberts.html

[11] Ibid., Chapter 5, http://www.earlychristianwritings.com/text/didache-roberts.html

[12] For more on Williams, see: Ian Williams Goddard."Roger Williams: Champion of Liberty." Goddard's Journal. http://www.iangoddard.com/roger.htm

[13] For more on Wilberforce, see: 2008. "William Wilberforce: Antislavery Politician." ChristianHistory.net. Christianity Today. http://www.christianitytoday.com/ch/131christians/activists/wilberforce.html

[14] Justo Gonzalez. 2010. *The Story of Christianity: Volume 2: The Reformation to the Present Day.* HarperOne.

[15] For more about Lucretia Mott, see: 1998. "Lucretia Mott.,1793-1880." http://www2.gol.com/users/quakers/mott.htm

[16] Mario T. Garcia. 2007. *The Gospel of Cesar Chavez: My Faith in Action.* Washington D.C.: Sheed & Ward.

[17] Ibid., 31-32.

[18] MLK, "A Drum Major For Peace." http://www.inspirationpeak.com/cgi-bin/stories.cgi?record=133

[19] MLK, "A Letter From A Birmingham Jail." http://www.africa.upenn.edu/Articles_Gen/Letter_Birmingham.html

[20] Bishop Oscar Romero, *The Violence of Love.* A free e-book/pdf collection of Romero's sermons is available here: http://www.plough.com/en/ebooks/uv/violence-of-love

[21] For more on Dietrich Bonhoeffer, see the following website which is devoted to his life and legacy: http://www.dbonhoeffer.org/

[22] For more on Mother Teresa, see: http://www.motherteresa.org/

Chapter 16

[1] As a side note, I love the New Sanctuary Movement. As part of this movement, churches provide literal "sanctuary" for undocumented immigrants who are threatened to be unjustly deported. In addition to providing them with food, shelter, and clothing, they hire outstanding attorneys to represent them in their deportation hearings.

[2] To learn more about homelessness in America, see: National Alliance to End Homelessness. "The State of Homelessness in America 2013." http://www.endhomelessness.org/library/entry/the-state-of-homelessness-2013

[3] To learn more about the global water crisis, see: World Health Organization. "Water Sanitation and Health." http://www.who.int/water_sanitation_health/mdg1/en/

[4] To learn more about global hunger, see: Hunger Notes. "2013 World Hunger and Poverty Facts and Statistics." http://www.worldhunger.org/articles/Learn/world%20hunger%20facts%202002.htm

[5] For more on the global burden of disease, see: World Health Organization. "Global Burden of Disease." http://www.who.int/topics/global_burden_of_disease/en/

[6] For more on this profound justice gap, see: Legal Services Corporation. 2009. "Documenting the Justice Gap in America : The Current Unmet Civil Legal Needs of Low-Income Americans." www.lsc.gov/JusticeGap.pdf

Made in the USA
Middletown, DE
22 July 2020